Your Identity:

Protecting Your Identity
involving
Real Estate and Mortgages

(British Columbia)

George Greenwood

with Winona Reinsma

i

Part of the

Keeping *Your* Identity Safe

Book Series

#7

Mongeo Publishing

Mongeo Publishing
165 – 20388 Fraser Highway
Langley, BC
Canada V3A 4G1

Editor: Monica Coburn
Artwork: Monica Coburn

Library and Archives Canada
Cataloguing in Publication Data

Greenwood, George, 1950 –
Keeping Your Identity Safe (Series) / George Greenwood
Your Identity: Protecting Your Identity Involving Real Estate and Mortgages (BC)
With Winona Reinsma
ISBN 978-0-9938214-2-4

You can only hit your target when your thinking
is clear and your concentration is sharp...
and you know what you are aiming for!

George Greenwood

If there is only one case...
and you are the victim...
That is one case too many!

George Greenwood

Disclaimer

There are those that will challenge what is contained on these pages, and that is a good thing.

It has taken more than two and half years to compile the content. Everything written within these pages is based on truth, real cases and experiences of actual people. The attention to accuracy and detail has been of paramount concern.

However, whether the contents are true or false is not the matter for discussion here. What is important is that this book and its contents cause you to take a good solid look at your circumstances. Then, you can personally evaluate what protections you should put into motion so that you can best look after your real estate properties and financial interests.

CONTENTS

British Columbia, Canada Edition

CHAPTER

An Informed Community
is a Safer Community

STOLEN *Lives* ™

PURPOSE:

The journey began with a long-term vision. The basis of that vision soon became the driving mission statement, and after speaking to audiences across this vast and wonderful country, I soon discovered that these simple words grew into my purpose.

"An Informed Community is a Safer Community"

This, under the banner of "Stolen Lives"™, became the "Keeping Your Identity Safe" series designed to provide you, your family and your business with needed information to keep you safe within your community.

My purpose is to show you methods that when utilized may assist in reducing your risk and decreasing your vulnerability to the various crimes associated with identity loss: theft, scams and fraud. (Identity Abuse)

The real purpose of compiling all this information is quite simple. It is provided so that you can learn to THINK for yourself about the subject contained in this book and that of the other books within this series – all related in some way to different aspects of abuse created by identity loss.

Sadly, it is a subject that too many people often sweep under the carpet as being not important, only because it has not happened to them yet. Hopefully, by reading this book you are proving that you are not one of those people.

Another reason for providing you with this information is to clarify a point. That is, too often the information that is convenient for you to find is skewed just to sell you something. What you find is provided to benefit the party putting it out first – and you second.

To clear the air, yes, I market services and products, but this book series is not designed to be a promotional ad for any of it. We are here to simply supply you with the information to cause you to think for yourself.

Researching and discovering for yourself is a better bet for your security and for your peace of mind. After all, the real purpose of this book (and the series) is to keep you from becoming the victim, or at least minimizing your chances of it.

Dedication:

We dedicate this book to all the current and future property owners throughout Canada generally and British Columbia specifically. It is our hope that you discover ways to improve the safety and security of all your property interests, especially your most valued purchase – your family's home.

We specifically dedicate this to all who may have fallen prey to problems related to real estate fraud or identity theft due to a fraudulent real estate transaction. It is our sincere hope that you can find your way back to having the peace of mind we were all meant to enjoy.

It is dedicated to those wise enough to realize that in today's casual world – anything is possible. The wisest of us accepts the responsibility for providing the security of our personal information, property, and identity.

This book is dedicated to the countless numbers of professionals that truly have your best interest in their heart as they assist you in completing that most important purchase or sale of your home.

It is also dedicated to those that have not been impacted by this crime – and may it stay that way.

Do not ever gamble with anything
related to your identity...
For it is simply all you have!

INTRODUCTION:

It has been said many times that life is simply a journey begun by setting out your first step. While this is true and we rarely begin life's adventure by driving down the biggest highway in the best of the world's vehicles, there is still no reason to begin facing the jungle by yourself with a machete in hand to clear your own path.

This is especially true within the world of Real Estate. To add to this, there are trends happening today that if you asked about, even a year ago, people's reaction would be simply: "No way!"

The real estate market is forever changing, and usually to extremes. We have seen an average real estate sale go for crazy amounts under list price, to huge offers over list. Money flowing this easily brings out the worst in people and the best talented fraudsters and scammers. Even the professionals say they have never seen markets like this. We have also recently seen the same markets drop because of conditions beyond the average person's control. So, where does this leave you?

You begin your journey by utilizing the information, knowledge and wisdom learned by those that have gone on before you – to many this is considered to be the best definition of real intelligence. Wisdom is often defined as the ability to use the information you gained from others. This series and this book specifically are designed to be just that.

These thoughts and findings come to you after an extensive amount of research over the past few years. The names of people and even names of businesses have been purposefully left out to protect their privacy.

The truth is, whether you believe the stories or not (even though I vow that they are all true) is not the important issue. What is important is that it causes you to rethink your personal situation and with the proper due diligence, causes you to seriously take a sobering look at your individual circumstances allowing you to make up your own mind regarding this important and often life changing subject. Oh, and by the way, remember that your circumstances may be totally different from someone else's. That means any advice received from that other person may not be valuable to you. All cases are unique and are often one of a kind.

I appeal to you to make any changes that will improve your future, your family's future and if it applies: the future of those connected to your business. I want you all to be safe from the theft of information that could have a life changing effect.

For those of you that say, "This cannot be all that big of a concern because I have not heard much about it". That is because the industry has done a wonderful job of keeping it all quiet. That reaction is what they want you to think.

Despite what most people seem to think, crimes related to real estate fraud are alive and well in

Canada and specifically, in British Columbia. This crime may be healthier in some parts of the country more than others, but don't kid yourself, it does exist from sea to sea to sea. In fact, rest assured that these crimes are no different in Canada than across the United States or any other country of the world. Real Estate crimes are close to being in epidemic proportions, and the innocent homeowner usually gets left holding the bag.

It has been suggested by some professionals within the real estate industry that Canada is quickly becoming a global trendsetter in the ever-growing business of title or mortgage fraud, which is an upscale version of identity theft. The criminal steals the identity of the homeowner, and then proceeds to deal with the property as if it were his or her own. One thing is certain, nothing will change until our nation's banks work with the legislators to make necessary changes instead of sweeping it all under the proverbial carpet. Only with the appropriate pressure will the laws change and the necessary actions be put into play.

This is truly a worldwide problem, but it must start here in our own backyard.

I have collected stories from the United States, Great Britain, Australia and around Europe, but for the sake of this book, we are centering in and focusing on British Columbia.

Our land registry system relies on people being who they say they are and that they have the right to sell or place mortgages on the property they say they own. "How can fraud take place?" you ask. Take a sophisticated fraudster, provide him/her with what looks like the appropriate documentation, add some technology, and throw in some knowledge of how the system works and well...look out!

Some people have suggested to me that the books I have written, the seminars and workshops I have facilitated and even the media interviews I have been asked to participate in are all designed to set a mood of fear-mongering. This could not be further from the truth.

From the beginning, I have always said that I am not here to frighten or to sensationalize this topic. I am here to shock you enough to cause you to question your own circumstances in the hope that you implement some of the strategies that you will learn from my research.

According to one of the title insurance companies, "Incidents of real estate fraud (including titles and mortgages) are increasing in Canada." They go on to say that, "Those involved as victims are proving to be irresistible targets, therefore the methods of detection to be able to fight off such frauds, thefts and scams and to protect one's own interests are also increasing.

Think of it this way: Identity theft and financial fraud have increased over the past few years, not just in Canada but around the entire world. There are several reasons for this but suffice to say the increase of information availability and the vast growth in technology should have something to with it.

George Greenwood

FORWARD:

Technology has put miracles in the palm of our hands. We, as the general population (even our little kids), now have greater reach and access to communicational devices than even the American President had just twenty years ago. These technological innovations have had a great impact on us all, especially on the financial world. We have access to information unheard of in the 70s, 80s, and even the 90s. We can now do anything from trading stocks, checking our bank balances, pay bills, check our credit history, and transfer money online in mere seconds. We even think nothing of performing these tasks with total mobility from our telephones and now, even our wrist watches.

However, this great innovation has also allowed greater ease of access to our private information, our assets, and our identity to those who have criminal intent. It is also relatively easy to duplicate, alter or falsify documents with today's available software along with a little bit of skill and knowledge.

Protection is an ever-increasing industry, with a plethora of insurance options available to us. When we look at the real estate and financing industry, sadly these are options often confused, misunderstood, or just ignored.

Though many will argue that consumers are very well protected by our system in British Columbia, this book brings up many points to consider. Yes, to the most part we are protected, but often there are gaps that could very easily be closed if only we, as the consumer, had the right awareness and knowledge.

As George Bernard Shaw said, "Beware of false knowledge; it is more dangerous than ignorance." This is true in real estate where often people assume that they are fully protected with the standard status quo. Thus, they don't ask enough questions or do their own due diligence. While your neighbor may be fine with the standard protection vehicles or procedures, perhaps you see the value or a need for a few extra steps of precaution. Only you can decide what is plausible, after you have reviewed all the options and gained the suggestions and options found within these pages.

Awareness and knowledge is the key. We bring to light some interesting facts for you to consider and some clarifications of different types of protection that you might not have known about. Perhaps this is a great place to start your due diligence.

Winona Reinsma

Gone are the days when you can say...
"I have always done it that way and
it has always served me well."
Accept that the times have changed
and so have the way things get done!

Within the current British Columbia political climate there is an ongoing discussion regarding possible international money laundering. It is one of the reasons why the new non-resident withholding tax was implemented August, 2016.

The contents found within these pages goes much deeper than that. Within these pages, you will see examples of criminal intent and circumstances causing direct losses impacting victims and created by perpetrators that know what they are doing.

Remember, at the end of the day, it is your signature that gives you the responsibility for what you attach it to. It is always in your best interest to make sure everything is in order. Truth is, that is your responsibility and yours alone.

Prevention always reigns...
hands down.

CHAPTER 1

Safe-Guarding & Protecting Your Financial Identity

Once upon a time there was a family that worked hard and long so they could have the lifestyle of their choosing. They diligently went through their daily routines and saved for a down payment on the castle of their dreams - and such a wonderful castle it was. They were so proud because Mom and Dad, as well as the kids finally felt safe and secure. All their friends and family regularly came to visit.

This could be a story you are more than familiar with; could it even be your story?

Scattered throughout the house were the family photographs, souvenirs and treasures that were collected over the years. All proudly displayed for everyone to enjoy. No room for doubt that life is so wonderful because, after all, isn't this what we all want? The classic… "North American Dream"!

As much as you might say "Acquiring the house is just a dream"…Isn't that dream what drives us all?

Acquiring the ownership of that first home…your dream home, is the biggest goal for most of us. Then when lifestyles and the family dynamic change, your dream becomes the reason to move your household to a different location, often bigger, often in better or closer neighbourhoods and/or with better views. Reality always wins! To do this you need to acquire a bigger mortgage.

Right before your eyes… the dream of purchasing this magical home transforms into the dream of paying it off. After all, isn't your home your castle? The home may be the castle but the mortgage is the mote around it, and it often takes more care to deal with than the house. So, your question becomes "How can I be mortgage free?"

It is true that some people fail to even consider the very possibility of any threat against their identity or their finances; this includes theft and fraud related to their Real Estate. Truth is, this type of fraud collectively causes financial losses in the hundreds of millions of dollars throughout Canada every year. Identity thieves are constantly trying to obtain valuable personal data and with that information these same fraudsters can convert the property title of a home to their own use.

This can result in having additional mortgages or claims unknowingly applied to one's property, or worse, having the property sold right out from under the owner's feet.

> *   As a side note, please allow me to explain… The entire premise of my teaching is based on the need for identity theft prevention… the key word being "prevention". It is not about methods to fix or make the situation better **AFTER** the fact… prevention is about stopping the*

*action **BEFORE** the act even occurs.*

Without proper protection, identity theft or fraud related to Real Estate can be just as devastating to a homeowner as any high-magnitude earthquake or fully engulfed fire. The irony here is that issues related to these situations can often be relatively easy to safeguard against. This can be done by using any number of available safeguarding options making these situations even more preventable.

There are dozens, if not hundreds of homeowners per year in Canada that get victimized by real estate frauds. Various Canadian title companies released numbers in 2015 that were similar. They were staggering… between $300 million and $1.5 billion are lost annually to such frauds, with an average loss of approximately $300,000.

This is totally disruptive and damaging to those involved. It can range from the actual loss of a home to the need to spend thousands of dollars and hours of time to fight for your name, reputation and finances to be restored.

The truth is that every part of your identity, as well as your financial instruments, could be either a target or tool to a perpetrator. Like any business, there are specialties and individuals that excel using niche areas within their own operation. The world of the identity thief is no different.

Surprising to my speaking event audiences, I often ask them to: "Respect the thief" … not for who they are or for what they do – but for how well they have learned to operate their Business", and I do stress: It is a business, and many of them are very good at their craft.

This clearly means that personal investments, loans, property titles, business documents and other forms of your identification can be a target. Before we dive deeper into this, please allow me to ask you a question: "Who do you think is the most vulnerable to be a victim of mortgage fraud?"

My guess is that some of you may be relieved and may even have a sense of relief as you say, "I don't need to be concerned about mortgage fraud since I don't have a mortgage. Our home is mortgage free. We own it outright and have a clear title."

Well, Good Morning.... get ready to be surprised! You are the most vulnerable to become a mortgage fraud victim. It is easier to attach a mortgage to a home that is free and clear because it does not have any liens that need to be discharged first.

> * At this point, I need to provide the second side note. Before you panic, allow me to say that the information contained in this book is not intended to frighten you. However, it is designed to provide you with basic knowledge and awareness that will direct you toward the tools needed to place protection in the areas you need it most. It is intended to get you thinking about your individual

4

circumstances and how to step toward improving them.

Please realize that your first line of defense is your own expanded awareness and your willingness to accept the fact that mortgage fraud is real and could happen (yes, even to you). This, believe it or not, is your first step towards being protected. Then having you inspect your individual circumstances from a different set of lenses. This will allow you to clearly see what areas are vulnerably open and require more attention, and of course, protection.

Typically, our human nature or our controlling ego mind almost always wants to step in here... but my research reveals three human truths that we rarely care to acknowledge, discuss or understand.

These are:

1. **"We do what we do"** Our habits, our built-in patterns, our culture, our heritage and even our routines that we have built up over the years cause us to fall into a repetitive state that we unconsciously follow because "we are who we are and habitually do what we do!"

2. **"We do not know what we do not know."** Obviously, it is impossible to know everything and it is impossible to keep up with all the constant changes that relate to this subject in today's revolving society. Too often we are so content in our thinking that we don't need (or care) to know the details any more. With an

attitude of, "what I do know has gotten me this far" stops us from doing our proper and too often necessary due diligence. I recently heard an Anonymous quote "Those who think they know it all are very annoying to those of us who actually do." Laugh if you must, but let's face it… it is the root of the stubborn thinking that can get in our way of learning.

3. **"We cannot fix or change that which we fail to acknowledge."** Probably the least thought about, yet the most obvious. We cannot deal with what we refuse to accept - knowingly or unknowingly. Think about it!

Alternatively, your reaction to this might come from the point of saying: "There is no reason for me to be concerned about mortgage fraud since we are insured". We will be discussing this aspect of mortgages in both chapters 10 and 11.

One rarely discussed aspect of identity theft and fraud is the vast gap in time between the action and the victim being aware of it. Too often the victim does not know they have been targeted until they apply for something or require a credit check. In real estate, it can be because you are notified of the sale of your property, even though you did not know it was sold or even being offered on the market.

Like any game there are rules and strategies of play. Go against these rules and defy the strategies and you generally lose the game.

You can go it alone and take on the opponent yourself or you can choose to put together a workable team of professionals and experts in each of the required fields to watch your back. The choice is yours.

The main purpose of this book is to provide you with a variety of strategies to consider. One thing for you to remember is that nothing found or implied in this book is to be considered as legal advice. You are, in fact, encouraged to consult professionals (lawyers, mortgage brokers, accountants, and realtors) in your specific region as each geographic area and jurisdiction often has different rules, by-laws, laws and procedures unique to that district.

If this book causes you to think about your individual situation and causes you to want more information as it relates to you, then our purpose has been successfully accomplished. Our aim is to show you why you need to reduce your risk and decrease your vulnerability in respect to your identity and finances, as well as how you can move towards this.

It is easy to push the concept of protection and the managing of your responsibility onto the financial institutions, the police and various levels of government. While there are laws already in place to "protect you", the responsibility to put workable safe-guards in place is solely up to you. This applies to you personally, as well as your entire family and often in your business.

You could become an innocent victim or even

be traumatically victimized, either way, the correction and restoration can be very expensive and time consuming to prove, never mind settle. No matter what you do or what strategy you choose... always ask yourself: "Is prevention not a better form of cure?"

You bet it is! In other words, steer clear of the problem by doing as much as you can to prevent the possibility of this crime from happening to you in the first place.

Allow these thoughts to work for you because you were diligent enough to put these suggested protections in place. After all, it is better that they work for you instead of you having to fight the system, as you attempt to restore your good name, your properties and your finances.

Something to think about:

Some people go through life relying on
their luck or good fortune.
However, when going against trained
and knowledgeable skill...
Luck loses every time!

CHAPTER 2

The Hazards of an Open House

There is a side to the real estate market that has always provided a sense of vulnerability to the home owner or at least for any resident of the home in question. I am referring to, of course, the practice of holding an open house. Over time this practice of opening a home to total strangers has been fairly controlled by a professional realtor who is well versed and trained in the art of distinguishing who is a legitimate and bonafide purchaser.

The practice of holding an open house began in Chicago during the early 1900's. The purpose of it was to improve how homes were sold by using a professional home seller instead of using those referred to as "curbstoners" at the time. These were just folks with questionable intent attempting to sell someone's home to make a quick buck. A curbstoner would simply stick a sign in the yard stating that they were open for business. Thus, the "open house", which meant the home was now open to anyone for inspection.

Let's look deeper into this operation. What happens at an open house today? First, the owners or residents are asked to leave the property and to go do something away from the home. In other words, "Go away and do not be in here while people are coming through". Besides having serious buyers, a typical open house attracts nosey neighbours and others who are just curious – for whatever reason.

Some of these people are looking for decorating ideas. They want to see combinations of paint colours, carpet and hardwood treatments and so on. Some want to check out lighting or plumbing fixtures, they are wanting furniture ideas and others just want to see who these residents are. They look at what magazines or books are displayed; what pictures are hanging on the walls... all in the idea of learning something about the people living there. It can also assist the criminally intended perpetrator to fill in the missing parts of a profile. It gives them the opportunity to get an inside look at who their targeted victim really is.

Over the years this has been comfortably controlled by the realtor. Rarely were there more than a few couples coming through at any single time and it was all openly stable, to the most part. When more than one couple were there, it was common for some of them to know each other. But this has now all changed.

Enter the present time, real estate booms come and go. The market can be super-hot. An open house would no longer attract one or two couples, but would attract dozens of them – all at the same time. The realtor no longer has control. It becomes like the $1.49 day at the local shopping mall. People are everywhere. In every room. They are in the house, garage and throughout the yard area as well.

Why is this a concern? The answer is obvious, both personal information and property loss concerns are eminent.

The result is a perfect environment for would be thieves (both professional and amateur) to step into the picture. You now have a category of looky-lou's that are not looking for ideas, but are looking for what they can get for themselves. Trinkets, jewelry, little pieces that hold value and can be easily slid into a pocket or handbag. Everything done and not noticed by the realtor who is busy with others answering questions in another part of the house.

Identity theft becomes an automatic concern now. Perhaps this perpetrator is looking for more tangible entities like personal information. When the person gets into the house they can find the details missed on the homeowner's social media posts. They feel as if they already know you, it is just a matter of picking up missing pieces.

It is obvious that when the house sells, the home owner will have a substantial amount of cash available. This makes the common cheque book, bank statements, passports, credit cards and other pertinent mail and documentation very valuable. That added to the details related to what they see around the house adds fuel to the victimization.

How accessible are the desk drawers, file cabinets or shoe-boxes full of receipts? You may think these are out of sight, but the seasoned thief knows where to look. Remember, yours is not the thief's first rodeo, as the saying goes.

Alternatively, perhaps the would-be thief does nothing other than look around to get their bearing on the "lay of the land" so they know it is worth breaking in at another time when the residents are not home. Truth is, the perpetrator possibly knows your schedule, where you work and more about you as well as your family.

As an example, shown on a variety of national television network news broadcasts, a home owner set up a series of surveillance cameras around the house. One of these camera locations happened to be his home office/den. The camera caught an individual going through desk drawers and closet. Upon investigation, this individual was recognized by authorities as being the "person of interest" that did the same thing in another home in a nearby neighbourhood.

What can you do?

Here is a list of things you may want to consider:
This first list is more dramatic.

- Use only experienced, well-known and reputable realtors seasoned in dealing with a crowded scenario at an open house. Discuss this with your Realtor.
- Suggest or even insist that your realtor have multiple members of their team on-site for the entire scheduled time of the open house. This would allow trained eyes to be stationed at key points throughout the home.
- To only allow a reasonable number of people entry in to the home at one time.

- To set up a series of surveillance cameras so that you have evidence of any wrong doing.

This next list is less dramatic and should represent common sense.

- Put valuables away and out of sight. Remember, "out of sight" means more than putting an item in a closet that may be opened as part of the prospect's investigation.
- Make sure that all important documentation, receipts and personal information are securely put away, preferably in a locked drawer or cabinet.
- Personal keep sakes often have no real monetary value but represent good solid memories. For the sake of the open house, put them away somewhere safe.

Every situation falls into one of the categories that I refer to as my Crime Formula.

This formula is: **G/D + O + A = C**
[**G**reed or **D**esire plus **O**pportunity plus **A**ction equals the **C**rime]

This means that each of these components are required for the crime to be successfully committed. As an individual, the only part of this formula you have control over is the "opportunity". If you make sure there is no opportunity, then the chances of something happening to you is minimized or even eliminated.

It is hard for us to realize, comprehend or even accept the possibility of a situation occurring to us within the confines of our home. So, therefore, the biggest tip throughout this book and all my programs is for you to always accept is:

"I Accept the possibility that it can happen to me!". **Are you willing to gamble with your future?**

As far as Your Identity is concerned...
Let's keep it to yourself
~ George Greenwood

CHAPTER 3

What the Industry
Does Not Want You to Think About

Whenever you see any documented writings from within this industry they often contain one common denominator. They want you to believe that everything is always safe, secure and protected. I refuse to blatantly call it a lie, but there are times and places where this statement could be a myth.

These articles say that all is well in British Columbia because we operate under the Torrens law. They go on to discuss the security of Title Insurance, Mortgage Insurance and all other forms of "protection". Please see beyond this "salesy stuff".

Yes, these programs do work and they do have their rightful place. However, as you will see in following chapters, these are all just that - insurance programs. Please keep in mind the difference between being reactive vs. proactive.

Hopefully, as you read through these pages, you will begin to ask yourself these questions: "Does the method I wish to purchase and utilize do what I want it to do? Does what I already have in place now protect me from something being able to happen? Or does it aid in cleaning up the mess after it has been created?" An ideal program should eliminate frustration... as well as I repeat regularly, "Reduce your risk and decrease your vulnerability."

To get an idea of the size of this market, using numbers supplied by the Bank of Canada (November 2016) the Canadian mortgaged real estate market is worth approximately $1,428 Billion. With 74.4% of it or $1,062 Billion being from chartered banks and the rest being from "non-bank" sources.

Despite these open numbers, much of the mortgage or title frauds remain hidden from the Canadian public's view... as if to say they do not exist.

In a report published in the Globe and Mail (Oct 30, 2015) it was shown that mortgage insurer Canada Guaranty notes: One in ten mortgage applications contain some element of fraud. Equifax flagged close to $1.5 billion worth of attempted mortgage fraud among its lender clients since 2013. Much of this has no criminal intent. This is referred to as "soft fraud", meaning people are doing it just to be able to qualify for a home on their own. Equifax even reported that people come in with fake documents attempting to raise their credit scores. Their chief privacy officer has reported that this activity has increased by fifteen to twenty percent this last year.

My educated guess says we would be flabbergasted at how many times employees of various lending institutions have allowed or even encouraged people to falsify documentation to qualify for the funds needed to acquire their home.

British Columbia's real estate industry needs

to remove it's rose coloured glasses and face the truth. In a day and age where the attention is being placed on the high cost of purchasing property, the high cost of risk is sometimes over-looked. We forget that when the market is high and properties are worth fortunes in cash and value, it tends to attract those that want to take advantage of what they see as an opportunity.

Some say it is because of organized crime, or well-seasoned real estate fraudsters, and yet another group just never even thinks about it at all. No matter what side you take on this issue, remember, there are always those that believe they are entitled to the low hanging fruit that is easy to pick, and why should that be off your tree?

This industry, much like others, will do just about anything to always make itself look good. I have had lawyers, insisting they remain nameless, tell me of industry levy fees designed to gather funds so it can bury some cases from the public's ear. When discussing this privately with Realtors I am told, "Oh, yes, there is lots of it going on!", but publicly the market is squeaky clean.

I have had people tell me that this whole discussion is not worth their time and trouble to be concerned about. Then when something occurs, they then say, "I didn't think it could happen to me", but more importantly, they ask "Who can fix this for me?" It is just another case of burying your head in the sand until it is too late.

Then there are those who love to quote

statistics. They will be the first to say the numbers are not as big as they should be to cause alarm. Let me remind you that if there were only one case, and you became the victim of that case… then that is one case too many, right? Sadly, we will never know the truth since these "so called" statistics are limited to what is made public and not the whole story.

While we are speaking of statistics, every crime has its published numbers and facts. When it comes to this crime, there are lots of stories, and every organization states that it is growing and that everyone needs protection. However, this is the only industry/crime that I know of where the stats and numbers (current or historic) are nowhere to be found. Is that because it never happens? We know that is not true.

Is it because it is swept under the rug so the real dollar amounts and frequency is hidden? Could it be that the industry simply does not want us to know the whole story? Some professionals within the industry have suggested to me (off record of course) that it would be bad for business if the truth were released. So, what is the truth?

Reality says that the truth does not matter here. Does that shock you? Please understand that statistics can be exploited, manipulated or created to prove any story or point of view. Whether it is 1 out of 10,000, 3 of 12, 4% or what ever factor you wish to use or refer to… there is only one fact that is important and I have previously dropped the hint. That is, if you are the victim, the percentage is 100% to you and your family. The rest of the numbers hold no meaning to you… and that is for sure!

I love the classic statement that says, there are three sides to every story. There is my side or version (my truth), there is your side of the story (your truth) and finally, there is the absolute truth.

There are those that will dispute this book and its content. I welcome that. As I have said before and as you will continue to read again before you finish scrolling through this. It is not about what is right or wrong, true or untrue… it is about you having the appropriate and adequate protections in place so that you can efficiently and effectively protect your interests, property and family – no matter what. Is it better to have a bandage or be careful enough so you don't need it? At the end of the day, what else is important? It starts by you understanding what types of fraud there is in real estate.

Real Estate Fraud: - As described by the Financial Consumer Agency of Canada, real estate fraud is not as common as frauds dealing with debit and credit cards, but the losses are usually far more significant because it could mean losing your home. Real estate fraud can be broken down to the different formats within it.

Mortgage Fraud: - This is a devious means of manipulating the situation utilized by a perpetrator to acquire large amounts of cash.

Title Fraud: - Like most frauds, it usually begins with identity theft, where a person's personal information is used against them by a fraudster.

Foreclosure Fraud: - This style can be incorporated into the other two forms of real estate fraud, but has some distinctive differences. To make matters worse, this fraud feeds off people who already are in a position of difficulty.

CHAPTER 4

Let's Define Mortgage Fraud

Mortgage fraud can and does occur when someone deliberately misrepresents information (theirs or someone else's) so they can apply and obtain mortgage financing that would probably not have been granted if the truth had been known.

Here are a few potential characteristics that could cause a case to be defined as "Mortgage Fraud".

This can include:

When the party (whether the legitimate person or a perpetrator) applying for a mortgage misrepresents the past or current information by altering what is provided in the mortgage application: such as their employment status including...

- Position held or job title
- Length of service
- Show that they work somewhere but do not or refuse to admit they are no longer there.
- Full-time or part-time
- Employee or self-employed contract
- How they are paid (salary, bonuses, overtime, an hourly rate or commission)
- The accuracy of actual income earned and not having it over-stated to "sound better".
- Legitimate references supplied

Further to this information, it is vitally important that the applicant be the authentic person or the actual purchasing group that they claim to be. In other words, they are who they say they are.

The accuracy of the information stated about the down payment is also critical. They cannot falsify the disclosure of the sources or the amounts of any required down-payment.

There must always be a complete and accurate accounting of all information required for existing and applied for mortgages, loans, liens or collateral and debt obligations. Nothing can be left out and everything must be traceable back to the source as written within the appropriate documentation.

Any false or misrepresented information can and may be interpreted as a fraudulent action. Therefore, all the details related to the property must be included, especially if it has an altering or reducing effect on any tax values or purposely altering property details or leaving out information to inflate the property value.

What the property will be used for needs to be accurately disclosed. Obviously, it would make a big difference if the intended operation is either legal or illegal. It is also important that a true disclosure show whether the intention is to use it as a rental property or as an owner-occupied home.

It could be thought of as a fraudulent action by adding or subtracting co-borrowers, especially if it includes anyone who will not be residing in the home and do not intend to take responsibility for the mortgage. Are they foreign buyers or local? This will make a huge difference.

One good thing was the decision of The BC Court of Appeal, in April 2009, which held that unless a mortgage is granted by the true owner of a property, the mortgage is invalid and the owner's title will be returned to its original state. In this case, the registered owner (who was not the true owner) obtained the title by way of fraud or forgery, so the transfer charge was declared invalid.

Another style of fraud is when a con-artist convinces someone with good credit to act as a "straw buyer."

A straw buyer is someone who agrees to put his or her name on a mortgage application on behalf of another person. In return for their participation, straw buyers may be offered cash or promised high returns when the property is sold. Often, the straw buyers are deceived into believing they will not be responsible for the mortgage payments. This can and does occasionally happen.

Either the straw buyer or co-signer often does not realize that they are completely responsible for the full amount if something should go wrong. It should also be noted that this responsibility will surface as part of their financial position if they should be in a position where they need to apply for a loan or some other obligatory financial contract. This arrangement could also be used by the organizer of the deal as a vehicle to launder money.

Sometimes criminals may use information gained through identity theft, along with a variety of forged documents to follow through on a fraudulent transaction. They will usually default on the payments of the mortgage they just obtained.

Borrowers who misrepresent information and straw buyers who allow a property to be purchased in their name are committing mortgage fraud and will be responsible for any financial shortfall in the event of default. They may also be held criminally responsible for their misrepresentation.

Before completing this chapter, there is another B.C. story I want to include. It shows another side to mortgage fraud that does not necessarily have criminal intent.

A well-meaning couple, that have a preapproved mortgage with bank "A", put in an offer to purchase a new home. Their realtor suggests that her boyfriend, who is a mobile mortgage specialist for bank "B", could get them a better rate. Before the deal was about to close, this mortgage specialist (from "B") called to say there was a problem with their application. He said the purchaser's job letter was missing some information, which caused the bank to look closer at it and potentially put the deal at risk of falling.

Because bank "B" was still reviewing the deal, this "specialist" created a new job letter and pasted on the letterhead and signature from the purchaser's employer. The "new" letter was then sent to bank "C", which called the employer to confirm some details, which caused the purchaser to be placed on unpaid leave and not allowed to set foot at his place of work while he was being investigated for fraud.

The case was settled out of court. Bank "B" approved the mortgage using the original (real) letter. Imagine the frustration and emotional rollercoaster ride. The mortgage specialist admitted that what he had done was wrong and quit his job. It was determined by the provincial financial institutions commission that the blame be put on bank "B" for placing intense pressure on the mortgage seller to sell related products to as many borrowers as possible.

Many in the mortgage industry say this type of mortgage fraud is a growing, yet an under-reported, problem. It is not perpetrated by criminals looking to scam a bank, but by mortgage industry professionals looking to help their clients qualify to buy a home in a market surrounded with stagnating incomes and soaring home prices.

> ** As a side note, please allow me to note... This is to say all or any mortgage sellers, either within banks or mortgage brokerages are dishonest. It does, however, show that they, like their clients, are human and driven by desperation at times. It does speak to each of us very clearly that we need to know and have confidence in who we choose to deal with.*

Any or all losses from real estate, whether title or mortgage frauds can certainly be catastrophic to the homeowner, both mentally and monetarily. Not only is the homeowner faced with the high expense of dealing with the frustrating situation in courts due to high legal fees and time delays, but they also stand to lose any gained equity and title to their home... not to mention the embarrassment caused by the whole thing in front of friends and family.

We have all been brought up to understand that a mortgage on your property is nothing more than a debt and it is our ultimate "North American Dream" to get rid of it. While this is true, let's not forget that our mortgage also has a certain value as a tool of protection, and that after we remove the emotion of it, our home is simply an asset.

Here is where the shock comes to most people. As we already discussed, but it bears repeating: "Who do you think is the best candidate for the trained fraudster to use as his or her victim?" The answer is someone with a clear title on their real estate holding, which is usually their principle residence.

Understanding this, always ask yourself this question...

"If I have eliminated my mortgage, what form of protection have I initiated to take its place?"

Chapter 5

Let's Define Title Fraud

Before defining title fraud, let's define what a title is. The "Title" is a legal term which refers to who has legal ownership and the right to use a certain (defined and described) piece of property or real estate. It could be argued that you do not ever own the property itself, but you do own the document claiming you have the right to it or at least to use it. Therefore, what the title says is golden.

Title Fraud is a crime that is alive within Canada, especially in areas where the real estate values are higher. As an observation, the group we refer to as the "General Public" are not as aware as they should be regarding their possibility of becoming a victim of a fraud. Especially one that could threaten the security of their home's title. Too often, a victim has no knowledge of any problem occurring until they learn that their mortgage has defaulted and/or when their home goes into foreclosure.

Title fraud occurs when a fraudster steals or uses your identity to either take out additional funds against your home or completely sells it out from under you without your knowledge. They, in fact, get control of the title by whatever means possible.

27

You will see as you go through this, that title fraud is in fact, a type or form of identity theft.

Title fraud comes in many formats and usually utilizes false identities and often involves inflated property values.

The more common type, sees a home or property getting refinanced by an individual claiming to be the owner. This is done by forging documents in the owner's name. The act is performed based on fake identities. The perpetrator then receives the mortgage funds from the lender and often disappears – all before the actual homeowner or principle property stakeholder learns that the transaction has even occurred.

Another type is very similar but with a slight twist. In this one, the fraudster, using forged documents and information taken through acts of identity theft, transfers the title out of the homeowner's name and puts it into the name created to match the falsified identification documents, then finances the property using a mortgage without the actual owner's knowledge and receives the funds. Like the first type, the overall purpose is to disappear with the funds.

In some cases, the title thief may also acquire a title to a property by utilizing a transfer document that is fraudulent and may even have created a fraudulent discharge document to clear an existing mortgage. Note – this step is eliminated if the target is a property held in clear title. This swindle becomes apparent when the real property owner gets notified by the bank that they have a court order to sell the home.

In rare cases the correspondence between the "owner" and the lender would have gone to the fraudulent owner by means I am obviously not about to describe here; however, you will read more about it in later chapters.

It is possible that this procedure could perhaps have included such things as notice of arrears, law suit notices and any other correspondence related to it.

Finally, what if the fraudster creates forged documents that provide him or her with the appearance of having the power of Attorney for the property owner?

The industry will have you believe that stories like this are not possible. However, whether these examples are true (which they are) or not is inconsequential... What is important is that you respect the craftiness, intelligence and the determination of "professional" perpetrators.

Simply put, title fraud can be linked as another form of mortgage fraud. It is about being able to take control and gain assumption of a property owner's title by a potentially criminal element using fraudulent means. This could by example be a fraud artist, organized crime group or even legitimate agents associated with your transaction acting in an unlawful or illegal manner.

The biggest problem with this is that the victims of this crime always end up with large legal bills while defending their title to their own property. In other words, the property owner may win the battle but lose a lot of cash and their sense of security. They also experience a mixture of emotions including: disappointment, frustration, embarrassment and loss of their own personal self worth.

To say the least, this can also be responsible for damaging one's personal reputation. Even if the court of law clears the individual's good name, the court of public opinion has its own way of holding on to rumours and so called knowledge.

Many people believe the current age of modern computerization makes registrations more secure. However, electronic title registrations and on-line transfers have made the whole world of land registry unrecognizable to some, especially to older land owners.

E-registrations have brought some dangers to the surface, especially related to title fraud. If one is only familiar with the older methods of traditional paper deeds and mortgages could easily fail to properly deal with some of the newer forms and documents. This is a reason to always work with a well seasoned and respected professional when completing your paperwork when involved in any legal or land transfer transaction.

It all starts by having so much information available through a few computer key strokes. Because of electronic land registries, property assessment information and other information being available, a knowledgeable fraudster/hacker can initiate a case of title fraud.

Some of these on-line transactions can include arranging financing and obtaining a mortgage over the phone or on-line, never actually meeting the person you are dealing with. Some mortgage companies refuse to complete any of these transactions without being face to face.

In this depersonalized world, mistakes can be made just because of the desire for transactional speed. There can be a variety of reasons for this, not withstanding the competitive need to get things done – leaving out some of the traditional safeguards like using lawyers or other professionals useful for this. All for the reason of not wanting to "Lose the deal". Be warned that there are no steps of the transaction that should be bypassed.

In this changing world, often older people can be targeted for these types of fraud by getting them to sign legal documents they do not fully understand. It is also true that many of our older population fail to have some of the photo ID required. In the recent past and currently, our provincial government is making changes in this regard by having our photographs appear on more and more of our various forms of carded identity. To make matters even worse, some of our older and especially those immigrated to our country have their names represented differently on various forms of their identity and documentations.

Taking all of this into consideration, deception is still one of the biggest tools used. Sadly, although rare, some of this deception has been generated by the very professional you trust when it comes to documentation that you do not understand. Therefore, part of your responsibility is to know the reputation of those whose services you decide to utilize.

What to do if it happens.

There are no perfect remedies if you have the misfortune of becoming a fraudster's victim. Should something happen to you or a family member, be sure to always file a police report. Remember that often it is not about the police report, but is always about the dated and written record of it.

To start the procedure, you can put in a claim with your title insurance company against your policy. Sometimes this can be handled by the insurance company and because of their investigation you could be paid funds without going to court.

If you have been defrauded, you could possibly bring a civil action against the known fraudster asking for a judgement to restore your title to your name. If the fraudster(s) have the available funds, you can also ask for possible damages from them.

Your real estate lawyer will most likely be your greatest allied force. With their experience and knowledge of procedure they will be a great asset in this time of grief and need.

It could also be possible to show that there is negligence against your lawyer. However, this is not easy to prove and obviously requires evidence. If you have become a victim of this, be sure to investigate ALL possibilities.

A couple of years ago, I had the mortgage manager of one of our major banks tell me that he has been approached, more frequently than you would believe, to be an accomplice or partner in real estate fraud transactions.

Another area to be concerned as a homeowner is if you find it necessary to defend yourself in a mortgage enforcement proceeding brought against you regarding the possession or sale of a home to satisfy a mortgage debt. This is difficult and can be cumbersome because it requires you as the homeowner to produce evidence that describes the validity of the very same mortgage you are being asked about.

You can also take advantage of British Columbia's Land Title Registry, which carries a degree of protection and assistance. It is possible to request that fraudulent or false information that has been put on title be removed. See Chapter 13: about the Torrens Law and Chapter 14: about the Assurance Fund Reserve.

Chapter 6

Let's Define Foreclosure Fraud

Let's first get to the basics. A foreclosure is some-thing that hopefully very few people experience for themselves. A foreclosure is a legal process that can be used by a mortgage lender to take possession of a property, such a homeowner's house, so that it can be sold to cover the mortgage debt that the owner incurred and has been unable to repay.

This becomes a situation that a person with criminal intentions can take advantage of by offering the homeowner a loan to cover their mortgage payments, expenses and to consolidate any loans the homeowner may have. In exchange for this "assistance", the alleged perpetrator enters an agreement with the homeowner to transfer the property title to them.

Matters could even become worse. Unlike a legitimate debt consolidator, this fraudster could even accept the payments as agreed upon and not pay any of the bills or taxes associated with the agreement. To take this one step further, the criminal then either sells the property or re-mortgages it and then leaves the country with the money. The result being that the homeowner lost their home and still is responsible for the debt.

Therefore, you must absolutely know who you are dealing with and use only reputable lenders in these cases. However, reality teaches us that the amount of risk one is willing to accept depends on the pressures and dependence an individual finds themselves buried in. The truth is, when your back is held against the wall, and there seems to be no other means to remedy the situation, even this despicable person appears to be an angel.

CHAPTER 7

Can the Thief Really Steal My Home?

The very thought of someone being able to steal your home is a terrifying experience, especially when you discover they used your personal information to do it. If that is not bad enough, we are led to believe that it is rare in this country and specifically here in British Columbia.

We are taught that there are already built-in safe-guards in place here. We are told that because of the "Torrens" Land Title System the possibility is eliminated - but it still can and does happen. There are professionals who suggest that the system is so well put together that purchasing further back-up is not necessary.

The same professional will tell you that if something does happen the Provincial Land Titles Assurance Fund Reserve will cover the real property owner's losses which were caused by the title deprivation. It is also thought that, upon proof being produced, the responsibility falls on the lender for not doing proper due diligence. To apply a microscope to this is fascinating to me. On one hand, you have an assortment of people within the industry saying it cannot happen and on the other hand... When you look up anything to do with this subject there are references to what to do if it does. How can that be? "It can't happen but if it does..."

When in doubt, I often like to turn to what I

call simple or basic logic and investigate it from that perspective. This form of thinking always raises a few questions, but primarily, if, as we are told, this style of fraud is unlikely to occur, why does the BC Law Society currently show 140+* publications about property, real estate or mortgage fraud in this province?

*(https://www.lawsociety.bc.ca/apps/lkup/adv_search.cfm)

Why does this same organization provide tips on fighting value impersonation, and identity fraud effecting real estate, as well as providing a list of steps to be taken if it ever occurred?

Why have there been countless articles in local and national newspapers and social media over the years suggesting the ways to avoid mortgage fraud, if it is not real?

For example, it was stated in a Vancouver Sun Newspaper article of February, 2012 that Equifax Canada, a consumer credit company, uncovered roughly $400 million worth of mortgage fraud in Canada during the previous year. This "eye-opening" number of files, industry experts estimate represents only a fraction of the cheating taking place in the country's real-estate market.

This article went on to describe that this amount of fraud was a one hundred and fifty per cent increase over the previous year. It is also described by the company's vice president and head of their legal department that "There is a lot more out there that just goes under the radar and is not seen or caught."

The *Criminal Intelligence Service Canada*, a federal agency which shares intelligence between police forces, reported that by tracking strong housing markets, discovered that mortgage fraud occurs nationally but is more concentrated in large urban areas in Quebec, Ontario, Alberta and British Columbia. Numerous criminal groups across Canada are involved in a wide range of mortgage frauds at varying levels, the CISC says, sometimes with the help of industry insiders such as property agents, mortgage brokers and lawyers.

If you don't yet believe this, ask yourself, "Why would cities and various municipalities around the Province show how to protect yourself against mortgage fraud on their websites, if it is not real? Why would the Provincial Government publish reports and handouts on Mortgage Fraud?"

On the surface, the answer can usually seem quite elementary. If someone has even the least remote possibility of having any control over your affairs, shouldn't that someone, be you? Simple, right?

This is especially true when it involves being accountable for your real estate property and other valuable financial instruments in your name.

Please remember, the purpose of this publication is to raise the level of your awareness and show you "How to reduce your risk and decrease your vulnerability". Think of it this way, by you being blind to the very possibility is the same as voluntarily multiplying the chance of you becoming vulnerable – and the same holds true to me. So, what is the truth? As I have stated previously, the truth technically does not matter. By that I mean, statistics can be used to manipulate, exploit, create or prove any story or point of view.

Again, as before and well worth repeating, it is easy to discuss situations that are "1 in 7", "28 out of a hundred", "62%", "only 2%"; or whatever statistic appears. When the real rubber hits the road and you become a victim, there is only one statistic that truly counts: - "1 out of 1" because it is "100%" to you! Nothing else matters. Please realize the rest of the numbers hold no meaning to you.

This makes perfect sense to me, but the question here is whether it does to you? So, let's go back to the original question: Can the thief effectively steal either of our homes? From the scenarios that are following this... I think you will agree that the answer is "Yes!"

> *Note: Disclaimer – These scenarios are based on actual published cases. None of these were made up. They are all examples of real events that happened to real people, but because of their personal interests and privacy... no reference is made to identify anyone.*

Once again, whether they are true or not is not the issue, the reason for showing them is not about the case but about you thinking how you, your property and your financial future would be safe-guarded against a similar situation. If you are not, it should be abundantly clear that you need to be. The point is that you put appropriate protections in place due to this ever-changing world where, sadly, business no longer can depend on the bond of a person's word or a solid handshake.

After you have read through Chapter 10, which is about your various protection options, come back to these scenarios and decide for yourself which one or more are most appropriate to both your situation and circumstance.

Scenario #1

It's getting late. The kids are asleep upstairs and you're just catching up on the day's events on television before heading off to bed yourself. The doorbell rings. "Who can that be at this time of night?" you wonder as you get up to go to the door.

Almost immediately, there's an insistent and rude pounding on the door. Now you're both alarmed and annoyed. You open the door and in front of you are two men. They inform you that they are taking possession of your house and you must vacate immediately. Not tomorrow. Not in an hour, but NOW!

This is a joke, right? But it must be a mistake. After all, you and your spouse bought the house almost a dozen years ago, and you've been faithfully making your monthly mortgage payments. To your shock and disbelief, these men are bailiffs and they are there to foreclose on your property since you have apparently ignored all the telephone messages, direct mail notices and letters pertaining to your delinquent second mortgage.

"Wait a minute, there must be some mistake here." you shout out, "I don't have a second mortgage." Later you discover that both the phone calls and all the mail were deliberately directed elsewhere so they would not get to you - all as a part of the perpetrators plot which gives them time to be long gone - leaving you to take the hit

It's no joke, no mistake. This nightmare is real. Somebody has mortgaged your house without your knowledge and disappeared without a trace. Since no payments were made on the new mortgage for many months, the lending agency is repossessing your home to recover their losses. Not only would you lose your house, but you are also on the hook for any shortfall between what the lending agency needs to recover and what they can sell the house for. Oh, and don't forget the added legal fees.

In today's real estate market, especially within British Columbia's busier areas, there are dozens, if not hundreds of homes sold overseas — sight un-seen. How hard would it be to include your home if you fail to have proper protections in place? It becomes an even larger possibility if your property has no protections built into it and is "clear title".

Scenario #2

You and your spouse are working in the yard to prepare for spring planting. The kids are running around and playing in the yard. You are excited about the new summer season coming because of your plans to further renovate your home. You are also anticipating the arrival of family you have not seen for a while. Then a moving van pulling up the street catches your attention. You look at each other and begin to question who on the block is moving.

Then you cannot help but notice the people in the car following behind it, as they get out and appear to be quite excited. You naturally think they are going to be asking for directions but instead you discover that they are there to move in to your home. Unknown to you, but they believe your house is now theirs... at least they have paperwork that says it is and they are there to move in.

You ask, "How is this possible? We never listed it for sale".

What would you do? Legally, what could you do?

One of the biggest and hardest lessons for us all to learn is that in moments like this, you simply cannot use your ego to bluff your way through it. Remember, these folks are there ready to move in. Their furniture and everything they own is prepared to go from the truck into your home at that moment. Yes, this is very serious.

Scenario #3

An upset renter decided to sell the house he was living in due to a disagreement he had with the landlord.

He could do this by forging a Power of Attorney for the owner. Apparently, the power of Attorney was in the name of the grandson. When the victim was asked about it, he said, "I don't have a grandson by that name".

Using this alias, the crook sold the house to himself (using a second alias). He took out a huge mortgage and then left the country with all the cash.

How you ask?

Good question... do you remember my comment earlier? When it is the thief's niche and it is what that individual specializes in... They simply just find a way.

An annual assessment notice failed to arrive in the mail, as they did for all his neighbours, the owner then contacted B.C. Assessment Authority and was told that he no longer owned the home and that is why he did not receive the assessment. He was then told he could not pay the taxes on a home that was not his.

The homeowner had paid off the home a few years earlier and was enjoying his retirement and told the Authority that he had not sold his home.

A year earlier, the property was assessed at $600,000 and the "new owner/fraudster" had taken out a $400,000 mortgage on it. The actual homeowner later discovered that the $2,600 per month payments were in default. Can you imagine?

This was a well thought out and elaborate scheme where the perpetrator transferred the property without the owner's knowledge and, of course, the existing owner was left off title. At that point, it was then sold.

The "buyer"/"new owner" applied for a mortgage and upon a successful transaction, the funds are released to the "seller" (usually a partner), which resulted in them both disappearing along with the money. This is usually only discovered after the mortgage company calls or comes looking for the defaulted payments.

In this case, there was a relatively happy ending. The courts ordered Land Titles to issue a new title to the original owner, but only after the owner had to look after an extremely large legal bill.

Scenario #5

As an example, reported in a 2012 article of the Financial Post

Using mortgage fraud to further other criminal activity is also getting more common. Criminals are buying properties to open marijuana-growing operations, to trade drugs and to launder money. An increasing number are getting caught and there has been a dramatic increase in criminal and civil forfeiture cases thus, said a lawyer specializing in loan-security enforcement.

He went on to say, "They're grabbing these properties left, right and center. And repeatedly they're crashing into the mortgage companies, the banks, [who are saying] 'Wait a second, we have a mortgage on that property.'" Lenders are losing big sums while governments reap the rewards of the seizures. Often the seized or forfeited funds are going into programs that are designed to fight crime.

Scenario #6

You sold your home. Later you discover that it had been acquired by a buyer who purchased the property by using, what turned out to be, illegitimate documentation. It was later confirmed that the purchaser used forged documents to complete the transaction.

You received all the funds from your sale and everything seemed normal. What you did not know was that the home was purchased for the express purpose of being used as a "grow-op" for marijuana or a meth lab producing methamphetamines. More often than we care to know, these properties can be bought and run by a criminal element and used for illegal uses and criminal intentions.

There are two sources of this type of phony documentation. It could be a result of straight identity theft or it could be information that is totally fictional. This is one of the reasons for the tracking of money laundering funds.

Scenario #7

There is a situation where the home is owned by a couple in a relationship that is far from being healthy. One of them decides that they are entitled to some funds from the home but does not want to wait for a divorce settlement to take place. This person applies for a mortgage to get the funds by using an accomplice to impersonate the spouse as they go through the mortgage application process.

This is a type of mortgage fraud that is referred to as a Spousal Impersonation.

Scenario #8

A home was owned by an elderly couple who held it in clear title with no known encumbrances against it. After they both passed away, their son was to act as the executor. It was time to process the needed paperwork and begin the job of selling the property so that the funds could be placed in the executor's account and eventually look after the couple's wishes as written in their Wills.

During this task, the son found bad news. He discovered that someone had already successfully sold it. During the investigation, it was determined that the previous sale was fraudulent. Now the legal "fun" was to begin.

Your first responsibility is to accept the fact: "Yes, it Can Happen to Me!"

Let's examine the probability or the possibility one more time. Some of these scenario cases can be rare and may never happen again the same way. The fact is that some cases of fraud against real estate have been covered-up by the authorities. Irrespective of anything else and like it has been previously commented, the thief just progresses on to a "new deal in a new way".

Again, the questions come up. How is this possible? Don't the culprits get charged for these crimes? Are there no stats published proving this? How is it that this is a low risk crime? How do they get away with it?

Earlier I asked you to respect the abilities of the thieves. Simply put, this is their job, their business, often it is their chosen "profession". That brings a degree of expertise into the picture knowing how they are dealing or even manipulating the law with any given situation. Today, both sides of each case can advance because technology helps anyone who has the knowledge or the skill-set to use it.

So, let's go back to the original question one more time: Can the thief really steal my home?

The answer is "Yes!"

Are you willing to gamble on all of the odds or do you want to protect your investment? The bottom line: This is your responsibility.

Real estate professionals often describe mortgage fraud as an upscale version of identity theft. It is a relatively low-risk crime with high pay-offs typically in the $250,000 to $500,000 range, but can amount to a $ million or more. The mortgaging agencies being eager for your business and their reliance on computer modeling rather than person to person contact, Canada has become the global trendsetter in the real estate fraud field.

The Quebec Association of Real Estate Agents and Brokers estimates that mortgage fraud throughout Canada, in all its forms, racks up $1.5 billion a year.

Taken down to basics, here is how it could work. The fraudster picks a property (a house or condo) to target and steals the identity of the homeowner. This, of course, can be done in a myriad of ways, such as stealing mail, rifling through garbage or taking details from social media. Most likely it is done by a combination of these and some other not so obvious means.

The fraudster then uses this found information belonging to the real owner to get a mortgage and disappears with the proceeds, never making any payments and leaving behind the obligation to make those payments in the real owner's name. This then becomes a legal nightmare as the real owner must prove that he/she did not take out the mortgage and that the documents were forged.

In the case of an unencumbered property— one on which the mortgage has been paid off—the fraudster convinces a lender that he/she is the current owner by using forged documents and forms of identification and places a mortgage on the property, takes the money offshore and disappears.

Another tactic is to assume the identity of the real property owner and then sell the home using forged documents to clear mortgages, generally to buyers from abroad who are not able to inspect the property in person. Then there are cases in which homes are purchased in the name of a stolen identity.

One Ontario woman found out that she owned a four-plex and a single-family dwelling in Brantford when the mortgage lender called her to demand half a million dollars in overdue payments. The thieves had used her identity—right down to her Social Insurance Number to purchase the actual properties and secure a mortgage on it. They then walked away with the money.

Thieves can also obtain access to a property by filing bogus documents, complete with forged signatures, claiming that the property owner owes him or her a large amount of money. The con artist then takes the documents in front of a judge and uses them to obtain a lien on the house and cover the debt. With a court order in hand, the thief sells the house, disappears with the money. The home's rightful owner has no idea that any of this has transpired until the buyers show up to take possession.

What about the BC owner who made the discovery at city hall that he no longer owned his home? He found this out by going into city hall to pay his taxes only to be told he didn't need to because he no longer owned the property.

What about the man who was to sell his parents' home and couldn't because it had already been sold by someone else? It cost him $11,000 in legal bills to resolve the issue and the fraudster was never caught.

How is this possible?

It has recently come to light, with the extremely high demand for properties, that bidding wars are happening due to the prospective buyers (which, in fact, could be a large group of ten to fifty prospective purchasers), all wanting the same property. This causes the "need" to have specific viewing appointments arranged and any inspections ordered will be required to be quick and given awkward allowable times in which to conduct them — if they are done at all.

On the other hand, it could be partly because lending agencies and mortgage brokerages in some occasions find it unnecessary to dispatch appraisers to inspect a property, relying instead on arbitrary computer research—called Automatic Valuation Models—to determine property details, including ownership, location, assessment values and other details pertinent to sale. Appraisal costs are always born by the client, so if it is not required by the lender it will not be done.

Were they to send an appraiser or inspector to physically examine the property prior to the change of ownership, the scam would quickly become apparent for what it is as the current owner and occupant will be alerted to the situation.

Having had personal experience in using property appraisers, it surprised us that we were never asked to provide proof or justification that we had the authority to obtain the appraisal. However, if a case of identity theft has occurred, the appraiser would have no real way to catch it if the lender has already been duped.

The job was fully performed, we paid the appraiser for the services and everyone was happy. It is true that some/most lenders do require the appraisal to be done by an appraiser of their choosing before granting the mortgage. The true expertise of the fraudster is to know where and how to get this job performed.

At times a lending agency may be over eager to extend a mortgage without them exercising due diligence and often ignoring warning flags outlined by the Office of the Superintendent of Financial Institutions (OSFI) or the industry itself.

It is not up to your mortgage broker to demand the use of an appraisal service. It is the lender's rules that apply and determine the need for an appraisal, which naturally, the client would rather not pay for.

In respect to a crime involving mortgage theft, it can often become the responsibility of the homeowner to prove they have been victimized. It is possible, at this point, to have the lending agencies aggressively pursue the most accessible target which just happens to be the rightful home owner.

Restoring your title is very time consuming and expensive — both emotionally and financially — but the courts are increasingly ruling in favour of the homeowners, they are citing that it is incumbent on the lending institution to do their due diligence. Part of that due diligence is making an honest effort to verify the identity of the homeowner through what is known as the "Know Your Customer/Client Rules" (KYC) as per Canadian Law.

Mortgage fraud is easier to do in some Canadian Provinces than in others. Some Provinces have stricter rules and getting around these rules is more difficult for the perpetrator - but not impossible. it is true, like in many areas of life, the crook will have the tendency to choose the path (or province) that offers the easiest way. In many areas, that easier path tends to lead towards seniors, but that does not exclude victims of any age.

One more thing: Do not think for one single moment that this is a "big city" thing. These frauds can take place anytime, anywhere. The size of the location makes no difference, especially since some of the transactions are processed on-line.

As I have stated many times and will continue to do so, we need to respect the perpetrator for their expertise – again, not them or what they do - just how good they are at doing it. To many of them, this is their business and they get very proficient at performing it. In this proficiency, they get to know how to either get around the rules or get you to – making you responsible for what probably would be an illegal action.

The Financial Transactions Reports Analysis Centre of Canada (FINTRAC) is Canada's federal financial intelligence unit. FINTRAC plays a central role in Canadas fight against money laundering and terrorism. Canada reported in 2011 that out of 29 cases involving money laundering in 2009 and 2010, only 34% resulted in a conviction. The same report indicated that many cases of money laundering go unsolved in Canada. Thus, the reason for the need to supply identity while transacting larger purchases with cash, such as real estate. The Anti-Money Laundering (AML) activities need to be understood by both the purchasers and the vendors involved in each legitimate real estate transaction.

We just need to realize this… Yes, the technology is helping the industry to spot fraud, but the same technology is helping the fraudster get better at what they do too.

With our ever changing and often over-inflated market, financially, this becomes more tempting throughout the province. Even with the new foreign buyer's tax factored in, the fraudster's selling price would just show it as a cost of doing business.

The best way for me to summarize this

chapter is to relate a story I often use in my live seminars. Picture in your mind, if you will, a one-and-a-half-year-old child dropping his or her face right into a beautiful and tempting chocolate cake. Now ask yourself... Is it the fault of the child or the fault of the parent for allowing the scenario to happen in the first place?

Here is the real question for you to think about. Is your home or real estate holding nothing more than this chocolate cake to a thief? Are you like the parent who allowed it to happen just because you were not diligent about the possibilities?

Are you so smart that you fail to see what is going on around you?

CHAPTER 8

How does it happen?

The quick answer is... Easier than you might think!

Today's Real Estate Fraudster is far more sophisticated and knowledgeable than ever before. They are often well armed with technical savvy and know their way around the internet to get what they need. In short, they know what they are doing and treat it like a business.

This chapter borders on me falling away from the integrity and the basic business promise I have modelled ever since the beginning. That is to never use a platform, be it speaking from a stage, penning a book or being interviewed by media, to teach someone how to use my information to become a thief. Therefore, I must twist this content so it does not become a "How to", yet still explain to you "How it can happen".

Here it is, as basic as it gets. As I just stated, I am not going to provide details in writing here but suffice to say there are two distinctive methods used by these talented perpetrators.

1. To forge documents that show a different name on title.
2. To forge a document showing the authority to act on behalf of the existing name on title.

Both are blatant cases of identity theft and real estate fraud. The thief's purpose and intention is to get as much cash from the transaction and as the saying goes... then get out of Dodge.

Many of these transactions involve single homes,

titles, mortgages and a collection of different contact addresses or phone numbers. All of which, (you as the home owner) can take place without your knowledge. That is, until it is too late… unless you have the protections in place that are recommended based on your unique and individual circumstance, as set out in chapter 10.

Should either of these take place because protections were absent, there will be a point when the new mortgage lender wants to start getting paid for the new mortgage agreement… you know the one you know nothing about because you never applied for it. At least they think you did… on paper, which of course, is all news to you. Oh, and remember the industry does not want you to think about this possibility. Just look at some of the examples shown in previous chapters.

The obvious question from this is, "Does the involved lender do a title search?" The answer is of course …Yes, they do. However, the well-trained fraudster knows how to get around this and disappears into the wind.

But wait… you say. There are documents at various levels of the transaction. This is generally true, but what if the documents that are used to check on are also forged in preparation or anticipation of the search. The search can be verified by referring to other forged documents. One thing is a sure thing; tell a fraudster it can't be done and their creative juices will find a way.

It should be noted here that this is one of the concerns in the discussions involving off-shore sight-unseen sales by foreign buyers.

Between the financial burdens, the personal frustrations and even the embarrassment that is felt, it becomes a factor most could not even imagine.

If there has been a crime, it is up to the homeowner to prove it. No doubt that this activity of restoring your title will be expensive – emotionally and financially. There is no protection in place when a mortgage is fraudulently charged against property. Title insurance is one way to create peace of mind knowing that your property is protected.

As the seller, if you are not working with a well-known licensed realtor, a recognized mortgage professional and along with legal representation, here are some flags that you can watch for:

- Potential buyers only produce a cellular telephone number and do not provide a physical address
- No realtor involved with the property in question
- The deposit or down payment you are given is not on either a pre-printed personal cheque or is a bank draft. (An added danger here is that the cheque or the bank draft may have been forged since the banks no longer certify cheques)
- Employment information cannot be verified
- The inquires and credit are inconsistent with the actual details, like age & occupation
- Purchaser shows the house to be purchased as his/her address.
- Inconsistency in the spelling of the details of their own name and address

- Transactions that are rushed or on a weekend when nothing can be verified

As the buyer, there are also some flags for you to watch for:
- You are denied access to the title or any title history
- You are provided with instructions to pay a third party
- Title shows irregular mortgage activity
- Be cautious and question the validity of the transaction if either (or both) the real estate or the offered mortgage broker have a direct vested interest in the property.
- Be wary if you are discouraged from using the services of an inspector or appraiser
- Be sure that your deposit or down payment gets put into a "trust" account belonging to the lawyer or realtor and not paid directly to the seller.
- You are asked to use the same lawyer as the seller. Note that at the very least this could be deemed as a conflict of interest and the lawyer could be brought up on charges against the Bar.

Perhaps you have seen the television commercial… "OOOH, you didn't use a realtor?" This is partly what it refers to.

You should never fall for the practice of signing blank documents or applications that contain incomplete or false information. Never allow someone in any negotiation to say, "To save you time, I will fill in the details later". Also, never sign photocopied documents with signatures on it since changes could have been made without your knowledge. You also need to avoid or at least be cautious when dealing with organizations that offer a fee for your name and credit information.

These are steps required to fight off mortgage fraud, which, as previously discussed, is also a form of identity theft that occurs when your home is stolen from under you by fraudsters who forge phony documents, which they use to either sell the property or obtain a second mortgage, unbeknownst to you, the true owner.

Albeit, we are focusing on British Columbia, but please understand that Ontario is one of the hardest hit provinces, with changes on the horizon, the provincial legislators are looking to raise the maximum penalty for real estate fraud convictions to $50,000 from $1,000. It is felt that this will also create tighter restrictions on how business is done, causing it to be tougher to commit such fraud. Ontario is also trying to establish a national data base of real estate fraud cases and to have fraud covered separately under the national criminal code.

There is a silver lining for those of us in British Columbia. The one place in North America where fraudulent practices in real estate are the least tolerated is in BC. It doesn't mean that it does not happen, just that the reigns are tighter and the fraudsters must work a little harder and smarter in BC. Our only weakness is not having access to actual statistics related to this crime. Remember... having no stats does not mean no crime.

Some say it is not practical, but what if as a suggestion to the Real Estate industry in this province, to have the property owner's photograph clearly shown on the title? Why not place the same photograph on support documentation, such as a mortgage, as well? This would hold true no matter what the position you are in during a transaction… whether it be to either sell or to refinance? The argument against this, of course, is what if the transaction is conducted by using a Power of Attorney or in a numbered corporation – or even with a group of multiple owners? Yes, admittedly there are bugs to be worked out – but we must start somewhere. Even if it is just done with private individual owners… it is a start, right?

The one conclusion that I come to is this, no matter what type of identity theft or fraud that we speak about, the one common denominator is that the naivety of people rings out loud and clear. Whether it be my old standby statement "I'm careful, it can't happen to me" or "I've heard of credit card fraud, but I never thought they could take my house!"

In fairness, real estate fraud in Canada, as big as it is, seems to be getting under control and less frequent (depending on, of course, who you talk to) – unless you are the victim. Then to you it is huge and the statistics don't really count.

Just because the market may seem to appear more secure is no reason to relax your need to put the proper protections in place.
In the end...

PREVENTION IS KING!

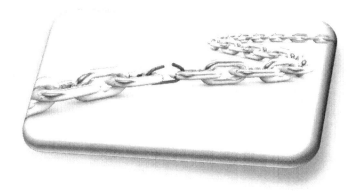

Our weakest link determines our true strength

CHAPTER 9

So, How Vulnerable Are You?

You are vulnerable anytime you enter an agreement where you are not fully aware of the area of expertise you are entering. This means that you must be willing to ask for and accept advice from those that have successfully gone on before you.

How do you go about protecting yourself against a variety of real estate frauds and various thefts related to your real estate holdings?

The first step is one I can never say enough. You need to realize and admit that these situations can happen… even to you. After recognizing this, there are six options that I will describe for you in the next chapter. Your task, with proper professional advice, is to determine which method is best for your individual situation. However, before going there, let's look at some ways to prepare for that decision.

No one ever wants to reveal their vulnerability. However, the real question to stop to realize and acknowledge is how strong or weak your vulnerability is. For some of us… this is the most difficult part of this learning curve. That considered there are a few valuable points I would like you to understand first.

When either purchasing or selling a property, pay attention to unusual practices that might be a signal that something is not right.

Question anything that feels wrong and, if you're not happy with the answer, walk away from the deal. No bargain, no matter how good it seems is worth the headache of sitting in the middle of a property ownership dispute.

Trust your instincts or if I may... your "gut". Did you know your gut houses neurons like those found in your brain? Think about it. How many times have you ignored what we call a "gut feeling" only to wish later that you had? If your instinct tells you something is wrong – it generally is. Or perhaps with due diligence you prove it to be correct enough to proceed. Better to lean on the side of caution than regret, as my late grandmother taught me.

Many questionable situations may show up on deals that are legitimate. This does not make it a bad deal. For instance, many properties change hands without the use of realtors. When dealing in this field without professional guidance, especially if you are inexperienced, may not be as much of a savings as you might think. Truth is, it could be much costlier. The trained professionals know what red flags to watch for. Understand that a few hundred dollars in savings now can translate into thousands of dollars' worth of frustration and trouble later.

If you think you have questions about something that causes these red flags to pop up in your mind – consult a professional. Remember, when it comes to your security and safety, the only "dumb" question is the one you fail to ask.

Vulnerability comes from several areas. Typically, the biggest stories seem to involve seniors. This is often because of two things, one being the trusting attitude they were brought up to cherish and the use of technology that is faster and beyond their comprehension. They may have the needed life experience but strongly lack in the speed of today's technical world.

Opposite in the spectrum is the inexperience of youth, which also tends to create vulnerability. When experience with large purchases and legal dealings is absent the red flags of danger fail to be recognized. These people may be technically savvy but their inexperience with life prevails.

There is a third group where vulnerability shines its nasty light. This one affects the group in between the youth and seniors. This one is like the last but goes even deeper into the ego of some people.

These folks believe they are stronger and above any fraudsters ability to con or take advantage of them. To some experienced perpetrators, these cocky folks are like pawns in a game... making the outcome more challenging and even fun.

A victim, no matter who they are cannot "Big shot" their way through this. Vulnerability attracts just about anyone based on an unwillingness to accept that "Yes, it can happen to me". Remember the first step in combating any victimization is the acceptance of the possibility of it occurring.

You must always remember what we discussed in Chapter 1... "We do what we do", "We don't know what we don't know" and that "We can't fix what we refuse to acknowledge"

Despite our thinking, we must realize that we are all in this game together and that we are not playing alone. Even more so when we realize that it is not about what we do (our habits) but it is also about what we can do (our strengths). This is greatly amplified when we combine knowledge and understanding by working with a team.

After being around this subject for almost a couple of decades, I have witnessed that there are three things that cause a person to be victimized: Ignorance, ego and apathy. Accepting this will turn vulnerability into a sense of security.

Hundreds of real estate deals are made every day. You want to make sure that the parties you are dealing with are who they say they are. Fraud and identity theft are a reality when it comes to real estate. My purpose is to keep you as far away from that unjust world as possible.

My purpose has always been to Reduce Your Risk and Decrease Your Vulnerability

CHAPTER 10

You Have the Ability to Choose!

Retaining personal data is just something we do without thinking about it. Most us would never associate it to our identity or dignity. However, it is important that you realize two things: 1. It is possible to have a problem with your title and the identities associated with it. 2. That there are steps you can take to block, or at least slow down any problem with either of them before it is too late.

Fraud against your mortgage or title can hurt you deeply. Not only is it capable of stealing your self-esteem, it can devastate you financially and ruin the credit you have worked hard and long to establish.

If the circumstance is right, it can rip your home away from you, both as your family's residence and as an investment. If luck be on your side, there are circumstances that will allow or even assist you in getting your property back, but it could cost you a lot of time, money and mental frustration – and even grief.

Whether you like it or not, determining the best strategy to protect your property for yourself and your family is your responsibility. The good news is that you have options and yes, the choice of which option to take advantage of is always yours. Hopefully you choose wisely.

As you go through this chapter, you will read a variety of choices. Behind each door, you will discover a different strategy. Please remember that no single one is totally foolproof. Each one can be subject to human error or be subject to unique situations.

Each section will explain the ramifications of each strategic option, and for those of you that own your home CLEAR TITLE there are options suitable for you too.

Most property owners feel that Clear Title is the ultimate "North American" dream. However, in certain circumstances this is a misconception. Clear title can be your open window to vulnerability and can make you subject to mortgage fraud.

Please remember: If your choice of protection turns out to be your mortgage and you find yourself in the position to pay it off, it just means it is time to re-strategize with a new choice of protective tool. You are always advised to have at least one protective tool in place and never own a home without one of these tools.

Therefore, it is also important to consider all facts and circumstances to pick the superior choice based on your needs, and I cannot stress enough that it is always advisable to get proper legal assistance and advice. This is especially true if you own property in another province or out of country.

However, difficulty comes into the picture when you realize that no two situations are the same. For some circumstances, a single option is all that is needed. A combination of options may be better for other situations. Each of the options has its own advantages and disadvantages, but no option is absolute and can claim complete protection for everyone.

In doing so always remember that fighting to regain ownership can be very expensive and carries a lot of stress. Insurance covers you AFTER a devastating event occurs, while prevention works as a "firewall" for you BEFORE it happens. You need to always ask yourself if you want to be reactive or proactive? Or in other words, is it better to fix a problem or prevent it from taking place?

Our job is to inform you about the ramifications of these various options, and as always, I cannot state this enough… prevention before an attack is always better than the need for a cure or restoration after the fact.

A few years ago, Joan Huzar, while she was serving as the President of the Consumers Council of Canada stated: "Canadians simply don't know that real estate title fraud is an issue, and that there is protection available. Purchasing a home is the largest investment many of us will ever make. Knowing whether you have title protection or not is an important piece of information everyone should have."

As you read these options appearing behind the various doors, please realize that the idea here is to use these as a protective tool, not to turn your home into an active ATM machine causing debt. The attention is on the equal and safe retention of your personal data, identity and equity.

If your choice provides any potential access to any funds from one of these instruments, again…you might seek professional advice. While you may want to use this strategy to secure a solid and non-risk investment, it is not to create a debt by using it to buy something, take a vacation or treat yourself to that special "thing" that a surprise windfall would pay for. Also, be careful to understand if there are any tax implications you should be made aware of.

Remember, as it has been said a few times within these pages… "You cannot do anything unless you first acknowledge the need to do so".

Yes, you can choose whether you have roadblocks to deter fraud, or alerts in place designed to notify someone should something happen… And yes, it is also your choice to do absolutely nothing!

Before going through the various series of Doors [i.e. your options], there is a strategy that I want to discuss but did not feel it warranted its own door. That strategy of using Builder Liens. Although possibly effective, is not as easy (or even as sensible) as you might think. It works by having someone place a Lien on your property just for the sake of "protecting it".

Let's look at this a little deeper: As an example, let's say your brother-in-law is a contractor and you have him place a "Builder's Lien" on your home.

First off, there are time limits on the registration of such a lien so it would only be

72

effective for a brief period. Secondly, and possibly more important, when you give a family member the power of your home like that, what happens if you have a falling out with that part of the family? They can now control your actions regarding that property.

Just something to think about:

Decisions led by pride or ego can be your greatest source of Vulnerability.

Remember, every extra step in place
may be one a perpetrator
is not willing to deal with.

Door #1 – Acquire the duplicate copy of The Title Certificate from Land Titles:

Many jurisdictions have a system where a duplicate Certificate of Titles can be issued, but only to the registered owners and upon their written request. In British Columbia, it has been this way since 1979.

Some people believe that this is the easiest, most cost effective and efficient way to protect your Land Title against fraud, but it does come with its own dangers and disadvantages. It is also only one method of "protection".

If the duplicate Certificate of your Title has been issued and therefore no longer in the control of the Land Titles office, the registrar will not register a transfer, a mortgage, or a long-term lease on your title until the duplicate certificate is returned to them at Land Titles. In other words, both copies need to be present.

However, obtaining the duplicate certificate may not stop the registration of documents such as short-term leases, easements, certificates of pending litigation, or claims of builders' liens.

You also need to ensure that the document is safely stored, absolutely secure and is in a place such as your safety deposit box at your bank, most common recommendation. If this Certificate of Title is lost, stolen, or destroyed in any way, it will be very difficult (if not impossible) to conduct any transaction concerning the property without it.

Yes, there is a process in place that can issue a substitute title, but it is very expensive and time consuming. Yes, it can be an effective and less expensive way to go, but be aware it also comes with risk. It is important to note that if this Certificate of Title is somehow stolen from you, or even lost, all advantages of this protection will be eliminated and virtually tossed out the window.

Strangely enough, the loss of your duplicate Certificate of Title may prevent some fraudulent activity, but it will also prevent you from doing what you need to do, such as selling, refinancing or entering any lease. In summary, to complete a real estate transaction both the original and the duplicate copies of the title must be present. Failing to produce both ties your hands into a knot.

With these thoughts in mind, you may not wish to utilize this option, unless you can guarantee the safe keeping of it in a secure place such as a safety deposit box.

Door #2. To purchase and assign a mortgage as a registered lien against the property

What is a mortgage? It is an interest in land that is created by a contract between you and a lender, which provides security for the repayment of a debt. When land is sold, the property cannot be transferred to the new purchaser until all encumbrances are dealt with. Encumbrances are claims or other party's interests registered against the title to land and include mortgages, judgments or liens. Having any of these registered against your property will act like a form of firewall that must be dealt with, before the registrar will transfer ownership to anyone else.

Therefore, the balance of a mortgage must be paid out in full before it can be discharged from the title. Only then can the disposition of the property take place. Thus, this being suggested as a protection option. It is better to get a call from the mortgage lender informing you that your lien must be removed before your sale can progress. If there is a fraudulent transaction going on, your reply is simply, "What sale?" You have stopped it in its tracks before it concludes. Therefore, eliminating any possible problem related to mortgage fraud or identity theft (or real estate fraud of any kind) that may have occurred, as well as possibly diverting a loss of both time and money.

When the mortgage debt is significant, there

is a likeliness that any fraudster will not pay it out to take control of your land. However, if there is no mortgage claim, and you have a clear title property (free of any encumbrances), it's one less obstacle for the perpetrator to contend with. Thus, again the reason for concern.

If you have a clear title property, one suggestion is to obtain a small mortgage for the sole purpose of providing protection. Note - the mortgage needs to be small enough to protect and yet large enough to be able to be registered against the title. Check with your local mortgage providers for this amount based on your area and your mortgage lenders requirements. This is another reason to work with a professional mortgage broker because the services provided to you are paid for by the lender.

This option of obtaining a small mortgage (or in some cases a reverse mortgage) will generally protect clear title land from identity theft type of scenarios. When there is a mortgage registered on title, only the owner or the representative solicitors may obtain any information from the lender in regards to that mortgage. The discharge process can include ordering the payout statement, paying off the mortgage in full, and obtaining the legal paperwork to clear that mortgage from the title. One important note for you to consider is that many lenders have minimum limits of $50,000, $100,000 or even higher, so always check by doing some homework before going into the marketplace looking for that $25,000 mortgage just for protection. Also, remember... to be effective as a prevention tool, the mortgage must be registered against the property in question.

Although having a mortgage registered on the property may protect you from fraud there are a few issues to note. A small mortgage registered against a valuable property may not be enough of a deterrent for a determined fraudster. Also, there is always a possibility of human error, so just relying on a mortgage registered against your property, especially with a small or no mortgage debt owing, should not be considered as 100% protection. Also, be aware that you could register a second mortgage, assuming it is written under the standard mortgage clause.

In some markets, you may be able to apply for a mortgage and have it registered against the property, but then not receive the funds, therefore not paying any interest. This is rare because there is no money in it for the lender. If it were to happen, there would probably be administrative fees which should also include legal costs. If considering this strategy, it is likely that a registered line of credit would make more sense.

When considering a mortgage as a protection tool, remember that it is not a final solution nor is it foolproof. Why a mortgage? A mortgage is "a document evidencing a debt owed by the borrower to the lender". Registration of the mortgage in the Land Title Office transfers the mortgagor's interest in land to the lender as security for the repayment of debt.

Mortgage fraud has occurred by having names forged and documents altered. It is not supposed to happen, but there are times that it has.

Be warned that a North American cultural habit is to use the cash that becomes available. Remember the purpose of this option is to create protection and not to create debt. Put the money away or purchase an instrument as a safe investment instead of using it to take that dream trip or obtain that desired automobile. This is another example of where the use of an experienced financial advisor with high integrity is extremely valuable to you.

What if you decide to Not Process a Mortgage Discharge?

Deciding not to discharge your mortgage when it is completely paid for is not a fully qualified option on its own for protecting your interests. Therefore, it does not have a door of its own. With proper advice, it is just a short-term trick that a borrower could use, keeping the "lien" on title. Chances are strong that your lender might not like this idea, but it could work while you are changing over to an alternative option. There will always be a definite point where your mortgage holder will want you to discharge it.

Having your mortgage lien automatically discharged and cleared from your title after making your final payment is simply a misconception. You must still go through the steps required to remove or discharge the lenders interest, including paying the fee to discharge your mortgage. A clear title means that there are no outstanding claims or interests registered on your property.

Here is how this option works. When you pay your mortgage off – delay in having your lender proceed with the discharge, which leaves the lenders charge on the title. While this is not fool proof, it does have the capability of providing protection against your property and that after all, is the name of this game.

Anyone working in the system will simply assume you forgot to discharge the paperwork and should contact you for a signature before proceeding with the file closure.

If the discharge on your property is delayed, the fraudster would have to clear this charge before changing the registered ownership of your land. Even to a seasoned and knowledgeable perpetrator this maybe be a big enough challenge to cause them to go elsewhere.

After making the last payment on the mortgage, ask your banker to place a notation on all your accounts that they are to directly speak with you personally if there is ever an attempt to get a release of interest on your account. If you explain your reasoning, they can often be very helpful in setting up an alert that works best for their procedures.

If the bank goes along with it, it will be a way of being advised of an attempt to transfer ownership. It will alert the bank staff to check for the note on your account and contact you before they sign any release of interest on your property. Please be aware that there is no guarantee that the bank personnel will check for these notes, as it is an example of where human error can be a cause for concern.

Door #3. To purchase Title Insurance.

Purchase your Homeowner's Title insurance policy at the time your conveyancing is being handled. When purchased like this it is a good backup, which covers the legal fees and they will handle the fraud case for you should one occur during the life time of your property ownership. In today's market place, many lenders insist you have title insurance and will not disperse funds without it.

Title insurance is one tool, that in most cases protects the homeowner's claim to his or her property for as long as he or she owns it. Where title insurance was not purchased at the time the property was acquired, several Canadian insurers offer something called an Existing Home Owner Policy and is generally costs more. In both cases, the policy will cover damages suffered—including legal expenses incurred—should you need to defend your title to the property. However, this can only take place after the event of a theft occurs.

Purchasing a Title insurance policy is relatively inexpensive and it allows a homeowner or investor to have the possibility of being reimbursed for the potentially debilitating financial losses that can be incurred because of title fraud.

Prices for title insurance can start as low as $100 when you purchase it through your lawyer at the time you buy your home. This is purchased as a onetime premium payment and covers your (you the purchaser) property as long as you own it.

Note that prices may vary depending on the type of property, location and value of your property purchase. Purchasing title insurance is optional in Canada, but many Canadian lending institutions make it policy to notify homeowners of the availability and importance of it.

In addition to compensation for losses incurred due to title fraud, title insurance may also indemnify a property owner for pre-existing faults applied against a given property title, such as violations of municipal by-laws, encroachments onto an adjoining property, realty tax arrears, existing work orders, lack of legal access to the property and unpaid strata assessments. It could also cover such situations as forgery related to the fraud, duress, incapacity or even impersonation.

In the event of a new attack on your title, title insurance will not provide a reimbursement of the time required to get your property back. Neither will it relieve the stress received the time used or the upfront costs related to it.

There are a couple of things not fully understood by many people. The first is that there are two broad types of Title Insurance. There is a Homeowner policy that obviously covers the homeowner. It can last for as long as you own the property and is priced based on the property value. The other is a Lender policy which protects the lender's interest in your mortgage and is priced based on the mortgage size. This coverage is usually required as a condition of the financing agreement.

There are conditions where you can switch lenders and have your policy "ported", providing the new lender agrees to take an assignment of existing mortgage. Sometimes the title insurance will follow the mortgage to the new lender and usually with no additional cost. However, you need to check on conditions and terms subject to your specific circumstances.

It is an indemnity, meaning that you would recover the costs of the loss, but not the property. Furthermore, the title insurer is not required to pay you until all litigation is concluded and that can take months and occasionally even years.

Title insurance is, however, not a silver bullet. Be aware not to confuse title insurance with mortgage insurance. They are very different, as these pages have attempted to show. Simply put, home owner title insurance looks after the needs of the purchaser/homeowner, while lender title insurance looks after the interests of the lender.

The only thing they have in common is that neither one will prevent identity theft or a fraud from happening. It should also be noted again that being an insurance, they look after your interests only after an event has taken place and after you are cleared by authorities of being innocent of any transgressions and that you were in fact, the victim.

Door #4. To set up and assign a line of credit with the bank as a registered lien against the property

The most recommended option suggested by many professionals within the real estate industry is to set up a registered line of credit at a bank using your home as collateral.

This is usually referred to as a secured line of credit, or Home Equity Line of Credit (HELOC) as a general term, while lenders may promote their own branded signature name for this product.

The purpose for having this option in place is so that you get notified that the account needs to be cleared before your sale can proceed. That is especially important if you are not the one making the sale.

There are three major and distinctive advantages to utilizing a line of credit. The first is that it gives you access to funds any time you need it. This works wonderfully as a great back-up emergency fund.

Another advantage is that it provides a lower interest cost than an unsecured line of credit, which allows you to take instant advantage of investment opportunities.

Thirdly, this method allows you to have instant funds for short periods of time, a strategy often used by sophisticated consumers.

Just like any coin, there are two sides to this story. Whenever there are advantages there are usually some disadvantages to consider, and this topic is no exception.

The first one to discuss is only a disadvantage if you cannot control your impulses. Many people find it is far too easy to use the new-found availability of funds and overspend (impulse buying) because of it.

Some people find that the legal costs incurred to set up a registered line of credit make it impractical as a first option to prevent fraud. While others may feel that this method is inconvenient if they decide to sell their home, meaning that they must incur the costs of the discharge from your property after paying off any outstanding balances on this line of credit and this is done while the lawyer discharges it. Still, to others it is a blessing. If it is inconvenient for you then it is equally or even more inconvenient and difficult for a fraudster.

When they went to sell their house the balance of less than $50 had to be cleared to have the conveyancing complete. Had the sale been fraudulent, when contacted to clear the balance they simply would have asked "What sale?" and stopped it from proceeding.

After weighing out the differences, it is still the chosen method by many experienced property owners who feel that this option is a working obstacle against fraud. However, remember that a line of credit is not a form of insurance.

One last thing… An individual we know used it to make a small purchase annually and within the next month, they paid off the balance – just in the name of activity. This was done so that the account was not to be considered as inactive by management of that bank – thus closing or purging the account because of a lack of use. By the way, bankers at all levels will tell you that this action would never happen. While this should be true, I have seen it happen. Can you imagine relying on this account for protection, only to find it gone when you needed it?

Door #5. Title Monitoring.

With proactive monitoring and timely notifications, a monitoring service could identify threats to your property. It empowers you to block fraudsters **before** they can take control of your title. By adding monitoring protection to your existing title insurance, you are safeguarding your property with the most complete coverage available.

Proactive property title monitoring is a relatively new service that has recently become increasingly attractive to homeowners and investors. Whereas title insurance compensates property owners who have been victimized by title fraud, title monitoring helps prevent the fraud from occurring in the first place.

This service will monitor your title information and flag any activity at the land titles office and send you alerts. Thus, it will notify you of the first sign of any title activity. From that you can determine if it is fraudulent or not. In other words, if you instigated it – all is well. If you know nothing about any title changes, then you can notify the proper people that the activity is not yours, therefore fraudulent. It is a way to stay informed and provides you with the ability to act quickly if a potentially fraudulent activity should appear.

Working around the clock, a title monitoring

service and its immediate activity alerts (often sent by email) help protect your property title from fraudulent activity allowing you to take decisive action before any transaction is completed.

Services may vary from one supplier to another. So, know what you are purchasing and how their notification system works. i.e. If all notifications go out by email and you can't receive them – what is the point, right?

Door # 6 The Usual Option - To Do Nothing.

It has been said that by doing nothing at all the decision is actually being made. As sad as it may be, this option is one of the most popular. I felt it should be included because too often it is the option of choice.

So, the question must be asked, "Why is this so common?" Like many areas within the identity loss and fraud world, and as mentioned previously, some people are too often dictated and driven by either ego, apathy and ignorance. These people go through this process with the full belief that nothing wrong will ever happen to them, which, as I have witnessed several times, can be the first step to becoming a victim.

To take this even deeper, in an interview with a former convicted identity thief for a different project, he told me he actively searched out people with this attitude because he knew that no protections would be in place. So, by doing nothing and not being willing to accept the possibility of it happening, the tendency is to leave access as open as a large barn door.

Thankfully, many of them turn out to be correct and nothing discouraging ever happens to them or their family. Truthfully though, that is more of a tribute to their luck than their knowledge or preparation.

What this really means is: Do nothing and hope by keeping your fingers crossed!

So, which is better?

To summarize this chapter, always remember that insurance is a good thing to have, even essential in some circumstances. However, please be reminded that there are two distinct camps here.

In one camp, you have a variety of insurance programs. This array of policy types can only cover you **AFTER** something happens. Only after some catastrophic occurrence can you open a claim.

The second camp is one of prevention. Prevention stops or even avoids allowing any catastrophe from happening. Therefore, you are dealing with it **BEFORE** it happens and creating a system that should not allow it to take place.

The best protection still involves being careful with your personal identity. Is it fool-proof? No, but it does reduce your risk. Also, it does not hurt from time to time to go to the Land Titles office to check on the title of your home to make sure everything is in order.

When either purchasing or selling a property, pay attention to unusual practices that might signal that something is awry. Question anything that feels wrong and, if you're not happy with the answer, walk away from the deal. No bargain, no matter how good it seems is worth the headache of sitting in the middle of a title ownership dispute.

A final thought in summary of this chapter. As a reminder, many situations may show up on deals that are questionable. Always ask if these points are legitimate or not? This does not make it a bad deal – it just may just require clarity. For instance, many properties regularly change hands without realtors or professional help. Dealing in this field can be dangerous without due care and professional guidance, especially if you are inexperienced.

Understand that by saving a few hundred dollars now can translate into tens or hundreds of thousands of dollars worth in frustration and trouble later. If you have a question about something that causes red flags to pop up in your mind – consult a professional. Remember, when it comes to your security and safety, the only dumb question is the one you failed to ask.

The point of all this is that deals are made regularly. You want to make sure that the parties you are dealing with are who they say they are. Fraud and identity theft are real when it comes to real estate, just as everywhere else.

Is it better to stop something BEFORE it happens, or having to repair the damage AFTER it does?

What you need to know...

CHAPTER 11

The Significance of Mortgage Insurance

Before going any further, Mortgage Insurance must be described and explained because it comes with a lot of confusion and misunderstanding. There are different forms of it and each has its own distinctive purpose. However, all forms of it often are simply lumped into one pile called "Mortgage Insurance".

You noticed that Mortgage Insurance was not included as a protective option in the last chapter. That is because it is simply not a protection for your investment and title, even though many people still believe that it is. Hopefully this chapter will assist in clearing up some of these misconceptions.

Then "Why do you have mortgage insurance in the first place?" The answer is better understood when you realize what it does and who it protects. It does not provide any assistance or protection against identity theft or fraud. Its purpose is to protect the lender's interests and they may require it.

There are three distinct types of insurance policies commonly referred to as Mortgage Insurance. There is Mortgage Life Insurance, Mortgage Disability Insurance and Mortgage Default Insurance.

Often, you will be offered a package that contains them all. However, by law the mortgage lender cannot compel you to purchase all three as a condition of approval. They can require you to have default insurance, as well as the title insurance we discussed previously. This potential confusion could result in you purchasing extra insurance that is inadequate or too costly. This is another reason to consult a reputable mortgage broker.

Mortgage Life Insurance is commonly offered by banks when the mortgage has been approved by them. In most instances, they will offer not only life insurance but will also offer disability insurance as well. Both of which will be built into the cost of the mortgage. These forms of insurance, based on your circumstances, may have some inherent drawbacks or advantages that should be discussed with your mortgage broker and financial advisor because there may be a way to get you better value.

Let's talk basics. Mortgage life Insurance will only pay off your mortgage if the borrower (that is you) dies. Similarly, Mortgage Disability Insurance will only cover your mortgage payments, as per the contract conditions, based on a described disability causing the homeowner (again, that is you) to be incapable of earning an income. Both policies terminate once the mortgage is paid off. Neither of these insurance models have any protection against identity theft or fraud.

As the homeowner(s), it is often required that you purchase Mortgage default insurance to protect the lender. It is required in cases where a mortgage is considered "high ratio," meaning you are putting in a lower down payment and requesting more mortgage financing.

Though there are exceptions, and financing rules are always subject to change, it is commonly considered that a high-ratio mortgage is one where you have less than 20% down payment, thus requiring more than 80% financing. Note that this type of insurance is always purchased because it is a condition of the mortgage approval, and usually the one-time premium is added on to the mortgage amount.

When your mortgage is protected with default insurance, if you, the borrower, fail to make your mortgage payments during your mortgage term and it goes into "default," then the lender has recourse to go back to the insurer for any losses incurred. This makes lenders willing to lend you their money if you provide this added insurance protection. Therefore, you are required to purchase this insurance to protect them, not you. Clear as mud, right?

For example, suppose Ms. Smith purchases a house at a cost of $600,000. With a 10% ($60,000) down payment, she arranges for a $540,000 ($600,000 minus $60,000) mortgage on the remaining 90%.

For instance, let's assume the lenders cut-off point of the property's sale price or the appraised value is 80%. At 90% the lender requires that Ms. Smith pay for mortgage default insurance that will protect the lender against her default.

It should be mentioned here that the purchaser (that's you) will always pay the premium, which is based on the entire mortgage balance. In this case $12,960 which is 2.4% of the $540,000. However, this premium may be added to the mortgage. Thus, the mortgage in this example would be ($540,000 plus $12,960) $ 552,960. Please note that the percentage is just an example and could change.

In conclusion, the point of all this is to simply have you understand that each type of mortgage insurance, while having distinctive purposes, neither Mortgage Life... Disability... Default Insurances have any provision to protect your title.

It remains your responsibility to do that by whatever option you decide is best suited to your situation. If that means going back and reviewing the last chapter... so be it – go review it again.

Often Misconceived!

CHAPTER 12

The BC Land Registry System

Land registration in BC has always been maintained by a system for recording ownership and interests in private land since the times it was a colony, well before the province became a part of Canada.

The Land Title and Survey Authority of British Columbia is a publicly accountable, statutory corporation with a unique governance structure responsible for administering and protecting the security of the land title and survey systems in BC. The LTSA claim that they are regarded among the best in the world at what they do. As of January 2016, they maintained a record of over 2 million titles and over 2.3 million active registered charges on those titles. There were over 8.4 million registration transactions over the past ten years.

This registration generally describes a system of tracking all matters involving the ownership, possession or other rights involved in a piece of land. It provides an up-to-date official and public record of all transactions related to the piece of land in question. Therefore, the purpose of this registration is to provide evidence of title and to facilitate any transactions involving these pieces of land so that it delivers secure land titles through timely, efficient and inexpensive registration of land title interests and land transfers.

In British Columbia, the foundation for all property business and ownership is what is referred to as the modified Torrens System. It is designed to make transfers and land ownership simple and certain by providing a sense of confidence for both the purchasers and sellers.

The ultimate purpose of the "certainty" portion is to protect the interests of those legitimately involved and to prevent any illegal activity or unlawful disposal of it, and naturally there are differences to the way things are done within various jurisdictions.

The purchase of a home or any property involving a piece of land is generally the largest and most important purchase any of us will ever make. Therefore, it will generally include the services of a lawyer to administer the legal transfer of this property. This is referred to as conveyancing, which is the procedure that places the responsibility on the lawyer to confirm that both the seller and purchaser, as well as all those involved in between, are who they say they are and that they have the right to either sell or have the means to purchase so that the transfer can be legally and properly completed.

Over time, it required the ability to track the history of documents related to a particular piece of land and its prior transactions as well as various transfer history. This became known as the Deed System. It became a system where a lawyer could follow the prior transactions to determine what outstanding assignments, liens or encumbrances were attached to that property. This system, to the most part is still used in many jurisdictions in Canada.

As for BC, this modified version of the Torrens System, because of its conclusiveness, allows title to be "assured" and indefeasible. It is because of this assurance, which is provided through a guarantee that individuals will be compensated if they suffer a loss caused by an error made in title.

CHAPTER 13

"The Torrens Law"

Have you ever heard of the Torrens Law? Do you even understand the function of a land registry system? It is okay to admit that you do not, because most people I ask cannot describe it to me.

Better known as the Torrens Registry System, the "Torrens Law" is what the land titles system in British Columbia is based on. It states that only a person registered as the owner has the right to transfer or be involved in any transactions involving the legal title to the land that person is registered with.

So, who was Robert Torrens? He was born in Ireland in 1814 and became the third Premier of South Australia. His goal was to simplify how land and property holdings were transferred. In 1857, through the Australian assembly, he put forth the *Real Property Act of 1858 (for the transfer of real property).* His system became known as "The Torrens Title" and has since been adopted and used throughout the world. Transferring property by registration instead of by deed is the biggest difference between these systems.

Some say Sir Robert Richard Torrens, over time, modeled this unique and efficient registry of land on the experience he had registering the ownership of ocean vessels through merchant shipping laws.

Sir Robert Richard Torrens
(1814 – 1884)

Within the Torrens system, in theory there is no need for a purchaser to search back through all the previous transfer records. Instead, the same purchaser can rely on the accuracy of the name on record at the Land Title Registry. This is to eliminate the need to worry as to how the name on the registry became the owner. Within this system, the named person on the registry has the right to sell, transfer or do anything else with their legal title to the property in question.

The Torrens Land Title Registration System provides a sure method for determining and assuring title to land. Under a Torrens System, security of title is based on the four principles of indefeasibility, registration, abolition of notice and assurance.

Indefeasibility. A title that is indefeasible cannot be defeated, revoked, or made void. The person who is registered on title has a right, good against the world, to the land. Under the British Columbia Torrens System, evidence of ownership is shown by a registered indefeasible title which includes the name of the owner and the names of any others who have interests in the property. There are a limited number of exceptions to this principle of indefeasibility and these are listed in section 23 of the BC Land Title Act (see definitions).

- **Registration.** Registration in the Land Title Office is important because it is required to establish an indefeasible title. While registration is not mandatory in British Columbia, failure to register means that the estate or interest claimed by an owner cannot be enforced against a third party. In other words, a person with an unregistered interest is not protected against third parties who were not a party to the original transaction and who gain their interests honestly

- **Abolition of Notice.** With the adoption of the Torrens System, the principle of notice has been abolished. It is not necessary, in British Columbia, to make an exhaustive inquiry into the validity of a title or an interest. Rather, a person who deals with land is entitled to rely on the Land Title Register. A limited number of exceptions to this principle are set out in section 29 of the BC Land Title Act (see definitions).

- **Assurance.** While the Torrens System allows the purchaser to rely on the names shown on the Land Title Registry, there are occasions where title may not be accurate. The Land Title Act establishes assurance funds to compensate individuals who are deprived of an interest in land through the operation of the Torrens System.

There are a couple of things to note here. When considering this method, be sure to ask if the Assurance Fund (covered in chapter 14) will completely look after all legal costs incurred if it should be called upon to cover a fraud. The point to remember is that this fund can only be used at the point of last resort.

You may have noticed the words "In Theory" used earlier when describing this subject. From a fraud prevention point of view I offer this thought which may not be popular from within the industry. Before providing this thought, please understand that in 1857 Robert Torrens did not have access to the internet with his smartphone or laptop. In fact, even Alexander Graham Bell's first successful telephone call took place in 1876 – 19 years later.

One more thing... Before getting into this thought, I am reminded of the words used by my friend and former workmate Brian, who when in doubt about anything would ask, "So, how does this have an impact on me?"

In layman's terms, the Torrens Law states that the name on record is official and can be trusted. So, I ask you, does that mean if a well knowledged and capable hacker could electronically change the name on title that the Torrens Law would protect the hacker's change? Just asking... especially since transfers can now also be transacted or registered electronically.

As I stated earlier, there are a lot of people that will challenge this thought... and that is okay with me. Remember, me and my basic logic? Well then, answer this. If the system says frauds and identity theft through the system cannot happen, but in real life it actually does...

How can that be?

There are some lawyers and mortgage brokers that are convinced that the Assurance Fund is adequate protection. That being true, remember that in an age when our vehicle tires are built with the greatest of technology since the tire itself was invented, we still carry a spare in our trunk – just in case.

Please consider this question...
What is your Legal – Real Estate Financial
"Spare Tire"?

CHAPTER 14

The Assurance Fund Reserve

Some would say that The Assurance Fund Reserve is the best idea to be incorporated into this province's real estate industry. The concept of it is to have a way for the property owner to be compensated in the event of an unexpected loss due to any form of identity theft or fraud.

The Assurance Fund Reserve is considered to be an essential and integral part of BC's Land Title System. The purpose of it is to assist victims if there has been an error made by the administration of land titles during a transaction, within the operation of a transfer or to assist victims in their losses because of a forgery, frauds or identity theft related to the transfer of the property through land titles.

In November of 2005 there was an amendment to the BC Land Titles Act. This change repealed the act to protect the registered owner against actions by a perpetrator by providing actions for the recovery of their land. This change provides the registered owner(s) with "immediate indefeasibility" and was put in place for the occasions when a purchaser acquired property by using a forged transfer.

But wait! We have been told these actions cannot be done, so why are there safety measures put in place?

To clearly explain this change, let's look at these two examples. Before doing this, let's define the players in these two scenarios.

- Adam is the forger
- Bob is the property owner
- Chuck is the innocent purchaser with no knowledge of a fraud

The first example is what would have occurred before the amendment: If Adam forged a transfer of Bob's title to Chuck. Bob would have been restored on the title and Chuck would have had no recourse against Adam.

In the second example, which would be if the same action had occurred after the amendment: Chuck would keep the title and Bob would be entitled to be compensated by the Assurance Fund Reserve.

This fund, as stated already, could be there to provide compensation to those who were deprived of their real property because of an error that was created during the land title transfer transaction, either at the administrative or operational level of the system.

Before, what has come to be known as the "Extension", it would have been the responsibility of the claimant to show that an administrative error had occurred through some action by the registrar.

With this extension, there is now what they call contributory negligence. This means, if it can be shown that the claimant contributed to a loss caused by the Registrar, then the liability can be shared. In other words, the claimant bears his or her portion of the reported loss and then can claim the amount of that portion of loss created by the Registrar against the Assurance Fund Reserve.

Often the Assurance Fund Reserve
is considered to be an essential
and integral part of
BC's Land Title System.

Chapter 15

Identity Theft and Fraud in Real Estate

The question of basics always seems to appear.

- How does identity theft happen?
- Where can these thieves get your information in the first place?
- How do they obtain your private data?

My "smart" answer is that you provide it for them. When looking at the broad view, many frauds, if not most, begin as identity theft.

Private information about you is key. Nothing can occur with out it. So, where do they get it? The answer to this question is the root of this whole conversation.

Think about what information is freely available about you? Think about what you have both consciously and unconsciously posted on social media – in posts and within your profiles. Much of this is valuable and useable information. Birth and anniversary dates, friends, school and employment backgrounds, names and photos of family members and so on.

When someone acquires your information and then uses it without your knowledge or permission… it is identity theft – plain and simple.

Fraud (by it's very definition) occurs, not by possessing your information, but when they use it. In short, it may be easier for some people to acquire a mortgage by using your name and information about you than their own.

They find this information by going through your garbage (which is not a crime) – seeing what you threw out without shredding it, stealing your mail or your cellphone, phishing for information or hacking you on your computer, seeing files you leave laying around or even just listening to your conversations in public.

In today's world, just keeping an eye on your use of social media tells volumes about you. What you post, what you like, your comments, who your "friends" are and so on... never mind what you show in the "about me" section. Birth and anniversary dates, personal contact information, your recent (or worse – current) trips, children's photos along with full family disclosure, and so on.

As a tongue-in-cheek comment, most people might as well just phone the crook and ask what they want. We really do give it up that easily. Then we wonder, "Where and how did they get that?"

Please remember that when you tell a thief that something cannot be done, it is the same as sending them a personal invitation to try. The various areas within the subject of real estate is no exception.

Like any segment of our North American economic system, there will always be someone who wants to misrepresent the ownership of a select and chosen property for their own personal gain.

The "system", as wonderful and effective as it may be, has put steps in place to prevent the possibility of any wrong doing from taking place. However, if there are chickens in the hen house and cookies in the cookie jar, the thief will always find a way to over-ride whatever system of protection that is in place. This is the reason why I have always preached that the responsibility of providing protection and prevention rests on our own shoulders.

Yes, as you have read throughout this book... "It is up to you!"

Despite what we are shown, as mentioned before, my usual pattern is to rely on simple logic. We are told by all aspects of the real estate industry that real estate theft and fraud are not possible due to all the procedures and precautions put in place. Back to my simple logic: If this were true, and I wish it was, then tell me why the BC Law Society (as it is shown back in Chapter 7) has 140+ publications about the subject within its own website?

The system says that Lawyers and notaries' public always check the identities of their clients before submitting the documents to Land Titles. FINTRAC (as described at the end of Chapter 7) rules require all real estate professionals (brokers and agents) to get verification of their client's identity and follow a strict set of guidelines with it, which includes keeping all client information as well as everything about the sale on record.

Since April of 2009 it was granted by the

British Columbia Court of Appeal (probably because of the case referred to back in Scenario 4 (Chapter 7) that unless a mortgage is granted by the true property owner, any new mortgage is considered as invalid and the title will be returned to the rightful owner in its original state.

With all of this said, the fact that land title transfers and financial arrangements can be conducted either on paper or by electronic means, transactions can still be done by someone proficient at conducting fraudulent activity.

We are in a day and age where perpetrators of crime have hacked into confidential government files internationally, taken over billing systems of major corporations, been hired by fortune 500 companies as someone they are not and claim to be.

There seem to be countless credit card "factories" producing phoney credit cards in the names of a myriad of people from around the world. There are counterfeit identity cards, driver's licences, and more including items that are believed to be impossible to counterfeit.

So, if this is true, who is to say they cannot make or create what they need to prove their "right" to fulfill the transaction and get the deal completed... Get paid... and disappear with YOUR funds?

There is a part of this that needs to be further considered and discussed, albeit not pretty. It has been proven that some cases in the past, within both this province and throughout the whole country, have had assistance from some of the professionals involved in the transaction. A trip to the publication section of the BC Law Society's website will substantiate this.

Again, to say real estate crime does not exist or that it cannot happen, is like operating with directional blinders on.

Identity Theft in Real Estate

In the end, the choices I make
or the directions I turn are all up to me

George Greenwood

Chapter 16
Why Should I Change My Habits?

So many times, on these pages, I have compared our lives to a big old barn with the doors left wide open.

Once again, the purpose of this whole "Keeping Your Identity Safe" book series is simply intended to show you how you can close your portion of that barn door as much as possible, even though you may never completely lock it... or even want to.

We will never eliminate or eradicate identity theft, however, we can take the responsibility to learn ways to reduce our own personal and family risk as well as decrease our vulnerability. By closing this figurative barn door, we reduce the flow of information out of our various barns.

Like the rest of us, your habits are the dictator of virtually everything you do. Many of these habits are based on routines that you do without conscious thought. There seems to be countless accounts of people being defrauded for no other reason than by not paying attention to what is going on around them or for refusing to accept the possibility that they could be the target of a perpetrator.

**So, let's consider the question again.
Why should you change your habits?**

Most of us have been brought up to respect and use honesty as a way of life and we expect everyone to do the same. We trust and expect everyone to be as honest as we are. The fact that they are not is reason enough to change our habits. If you object to this statement, remember that all it takes is one bad apple in the world to find you and then it is too late.

It is terribly sad that we must base our habits on a single bad apple, but that is, as Jim Rohn, one of my all-time favourite public speakers, said, "It's just the way it is and when you get your own planet, you can do it your way!" We cannot change everything that everyone else does, but we can control what we do and we need to do that immediately.

Yes, it is true that the various levels of government should step in and protect us against identity theft, however, as mentioned earlier, it is our individual responsibility to step up to the plate to utilize every form of protection that is both available to us and affordable by us.

Finding your information can be a lot easier than you think. Papers, files or statements can be found too often because of what I used to refer to as… "our carelessness", now I refer to it as "our thoughtlessness".

Any of these documents can be enough for an experienced fraudster to activate something in your name. Some have even been known to pay for "their own" credit checks on various credit report agency websites. Once in, they change addresses, passwords and make it so the real person cannot access his or her own credit report or account.

Omitting the flowers and not beating around any bushes, after being around this subject for a couple of decades, in many examples I have discovered that **Identity Theft** should be more appropriately referred to as **"IDENTITY GIVE-AWAY"**.

Sometimes the truth can be frightening. Our habits assist the would-be identity thief in obtaining our information. Many of us might as well take out an ad asking what the thief wants. So, therefore, it becomes our responsibility to take a serious look at our habits regarding the various segments of our own identity and that of our family members.

When writing *"Confessions of an Identity Thief"*, I interviewed a young man, a former convicted identity thief, who told me that he would look for people that believed they were of no interest to potential thieves. Truthfully, they were the best targets because their "barn doors" were usually left wide open.

If you get only one thing from this book, let it be that you now realize how exposed your personal and vital information is, especially from the growth of technology and the need to transport information between offices and various people.

The three biggest enemies we have
against us are:
our own ego, apathy and ignorance.

CHAPTER 17
What can you do?

All we can do is provide you, as the home-owner, with something to think about and consider how you can take advantage of some of these strategies. Doing something with it is your job, as well as getting professional advice to verify that it suits your unique situation.

The sad truth is that many people take the position that if they are not aware of this, then it simply does not exist and, thus, cannot happen to them. This could not be further from the truth.

What can you do?
The first thing you can do is accept the possibility that challenges to your financing by a criminal intent are possible. No longer is it acceptable to say, "I have owned homes all my life and this has never been an issue." We live in changing times. Some of this is because of technology and some is created by the vast need for people turning to devious methods of raising cash.

What can you do?
Be very cautious and mindful of who you give a Power of Attorney to. Whenever you provide another person with a Power of Attorney that gives them the power to act on your behalf with your assets and even your life, unless the powers you give them are specified and limited to certain areas of responsibility. This is an area of law that too many people fail to understand and is the reason why you need to consult with a lawyer or other

professional advisors regarding these powers and who you give them to. Often it is easier to give someone power than it is to take it back... which also needs to be considered so that you always have a way to end that arrangement as part of the agreement.

What can you do?

The social media world dominates in today's world. Check on a regular basis to ensure that you are only represented on social media pages that you set up. By that I mean, there are no duplicates made to have your friends believe it is yours, but in truth the page is set up just to look like yours. Also, be mindful of what "private" information you are freely giving away.

What can you do?

As you refer to the "Doors" in Chapter 10, please remember that it is impossible to cover everything on these pages. All we can do is point out your need for better awareness and understanding to these situations. The best advice is to always seek professional consultation to conduct all financial and real estate transactions.

Some people prefer to say they can save hundreds or even thousands of dollars by doing this work themselves without such professional advice. But what if? That is when the nightmare begins. Personally, I look at it this way: Is it better to have a lawyer show you how to go around a hole (preventive) or is it better to have the lawyer put a crew together to get you out of that same hole? (reactive)

Check with land registry office for your area now

and again to make sure the title of your property and home is properly listed in your name. It is also a good idea to check your credit report occasionally to ensure that there are no surprising activities on it that you do not know about. We recommend either annually or at least semi-annually.

The best advice is to never sign a legal document unless you fully understand and comprehend every word. As well, never pre-sign a document so that the details can be added later. Remember a simple comma in the wrong place may not be noticed but will make the meaning entirely different.

Regarding fees, remember that a true mortgage broker working on behalf of an "A" lender does not charge you a fee. Their commissions are paid by the lender. Fees would only be charged if it is private funding or what is referred to as a "B" deal.

A deal could involve a fraud if they offer to provide you with fake pay stubs, bank statements and tax documents… all that could come with an extraordinary fee.

Next, don't be so quick to brush off what you hear and see regarding frauds and actions taken with real estate or because of the funds raised because of real estate. Oh, and by the way… YES, it can happen to you.

What can you do if…?
If you become a fraudster's victim report it to the police immediately (always, no matter how minor – file a police report). Also, contact the *Canadian Anti-Fraud Centre as well as contacting either two or all four of the country's **credit reporting

services. You should also report it to your bank and your provincial land registry office.

Once you have a better understanding of today's financial and real estate climate, you can then review all the options available and do your due diligence - after obtaining professional advice. Again, your responsibility is to decide which option best meets the individual needs best suited for you and your family.

* www.antifraudcentre.ca
** Equifax, TransUnion, Experian and Northern Credit

Take the action required to protect yourself,
your family and
your investment in your home.

CHAPTER 18

How can we help you?

There is an old story told by a sales professional about a lawyer who went into a business wishing to make a purchase of carpet needed to enhance and improve his office. The challenge this lawyer faced was that he totally lacked any firsthand knowledge of these products and was about to make the selection purely on looks and impression.

Seeing this, the salesman offered advice based on knowledge and experience, but these suggestions and offer to assist were rejected based on the inclination to make up his own mind based on his own uneducated conclusions. The problem was that this selected product was chosen purely based on appearance and not performance. Therefore, it was inadequate for the desired project and would not serve the need. In the long run, it would have been an expensive disappointment.

Knowing that this individual had an ego and stubborn streak, the salesman asked this question... "If I had a question about a health challenge, would I go to my friend the auto mechanic for advice?" The lawyer answered: "Of course not, you would see a doctor." The salesperson the asked "So, if I had a legal issue, would I go to a Plumber?" "Obviously not!", the lawyer replied. "You would see someone like me". To that the salesman asked, "So, by understanding your answers, if a person has a question regarding the products I professionally represent, should that same person ask their questions to me?" The lawyer stormed out of the store as if to be insulted, but a couple of days later returned and said, "I have been thinking about what you said to me. Would you still be willing to assist me?"

I tell you this story for a very fitting reason. The area of real estate financing is complicated and understood by fewer people than you can imagine. The same is true with areas of identity abuse through theft and fraud.

The two of us (George & Winona) involved in this book would be happy to answer any questions you might have regarding your individual circumstances. If we do not have the required answers you need, much like the example of the salesman, between the two of us – we will either contact the professionals in that area of expertise or we will direct you to them so that you get the answers you require.

George Greenwood
778 552 0961
george@keepingidentitysafe.com

Winona Reinsma
604 882 3643
winonareinsma@gmail.com

Chapter 19
The Summary

Thank you for reading this book. We hope that it has provided some insight to this often misconceived or even never thought of subject – until it is too late.

It is our sincerest hope that you never experience any of the difficulties that we have described on these pages. The trick is to keep it that way.

Along with this thought comes our desire to prevent you from becoming devastated from such occurrences and having the need to find a way to recover from it. By adopting an attitude of prevention and put an appropriate strategy in place you will reduce your risk of becoming a victim of fraud or devastating loss.

The best protection always has and always will involve being careful and mindful with your personal identity and property, no matter what form it takes. Awareness and knowledge will always be king.

Throughout these pages, you have read about both sides of this interesting coin. The rest is up to you.

Even though, we know this information to be as accurate as it can be at the time of writing, realize that laws and procedures do change. Each situation and all circumstances vary from deal to deal and from area to area.

It is up to you to do your own due diligence

making sure that all the "I's are dotted and the t's are crossed" in the proper way. It is our sincere hope that this book has at least caused you to see out of a bigger window and assisted you in knowing what to look for.

It is alright for you to question what is contained here and what the various agencies are saying about how safe it is and how situations involving wrong doing are no longer possible.

Again, we are suggesting that the ultimate responsibility of keeping your welfare and that of your family in order, is yours. Your responsibility is to put as many firewalls and protective options in place that you feel are necessary.

After all, your home and other purchased properties are without a doubt, probably the largest investments you will ever make.

Therefore, to provide the most cautious and protective care for it that you can is your responsibility.

When all is said, and done...

It's up to you!

I always close my live speaking events by asking the audience the following question, and right now it seems appropriate to direct it to you.

"There are five birds of equal size and colours sitting on a wire between two telephone poles. Three of these birds decide to fly off. So, how many birds are left?

If you guessed two, like many people do – you would be incorrect. The answer is five. You see they all knew what to do and three even decided to do something. However, they failed to take the action.

So, now it is time for the bigger question:
Will you just think about it, perhaps even do some research of your own. But, will you follow through by applying the appropriate strategies to your plan?

Our desire is to reduce your risk and decrease your vulnerability so you can always be...

The ONLY YOU there is!

Definitions:

Automated Valuation Model (AVM): is the name given to a service that can provide real estate property valuations using a database combined with mathematical modeling. Most AVMs calculate a property's value at a specific point in time by analyzing values of comparable properties. Some also consider historical house price movements, previous surveyor valuations, and user inputs (i.e. additional bedrooms, home improvements, etc.).

Appraisers, investment professionals and lending institutions use AVM technology in their analysis of residential property. The results of each are weighted, analyzed and then reported as a final estimate of value based on a requested date.

Fraud: is a deliberate deception intended to secure unlawful or unfair gain – personal or financial. Fraud is both a civil wrong (a fraud victim may sue the fraud perpetrator to void the fraud and/or recover monetary compensation) and a criminal wrong (a fraud perpetrator may be prosecuted and imprisoned by governmental authorities). The purpose of fraud may be monetary gain or other benefits, such as obtaining a driver's license or any other legally accepted document by way of false statements. *(get proper legal advice based on your jurisdiction and circumstances)*

Identity Theft: is when any person commits an offence who, without lawful excuse, procures to be made, possesses, transfers, sells or offers for sale an identity document that relates or purports to relate, in whole or in part, to another person.

As by definition in the Criminal Code of Canada, Identity information includes biological or physiological information — of a type that is commonly used alone or in combination with other information to identify or purport to identify an individual, including a fingerprint, voice print, retina image, iris image, DNA profile, name, address, date of birth, written signature, electronic signature, digital signature, user name, credit card number, debit card number, financial institution account number, passport number, Social Insurance Number, health insurance number, driver's licence number or password.

Everyone commits an offence who knowingly obtains or possesses another person's identity information in circumstances giving rise to a reasonable inference that the information is intended to be used to commit an indictable offence that includes fraud, deceit or falsehood as an element of the offence.

Everyone commits an offence who transmits, makes available, distributes, sells or offers for sale another person's identity information, or has it in their possession for any of those purposes, knowing that or being reckless as to whether the information will be used to commit an indictable offence that includes fraud, deceit or falsehood as an element of the offence.

Mortgage: is a form of a loan used by purchasers of real property. It is a way of raising needed funds, while putting a lien on the property being mortgaged. The loan is "secured" on the borrower's property. This means that a legal mechanism is put in place which allows the lender to take possession and sell the secured property ("foreclosure" or "repossession") to pay off the loan in the event that the borrower defaults on the loan or otherwise fails to abide by its terms. The word *mortgage* is derived from an Old Norman or Anglo-Norman term used by lawyers in the Middle-Ages meaning "death pledge". This refers to the pledge ending (dying) when either the collateral obligation is fulfilled or by the property being taken in an action referred to as foreclosure.

Mortgage borrowers can be individuals mortgaging their home or they can be businesses mortgaging commercial property (for example, their own business premises, residential property let to tenants or an investment portfolio). The lender will typically be a financial institution, such as a bank, credit union or building society, depending on the country concerned, and the loan arrangements can be made either directly or indirectly through intermediaries. Features of mortgage loans such as the size of the loan, maturity of the loan, interest rate, method of paying off the loan, and other characteristics can vary considerably. The lender's rights over the secured property take priority over the borrower's other creditors which means that if the borrower becomes bankrupt or insolvent, the other creditors will only be repaid the debts owed to them from a sale of the secured property if the mortgage lender is repaid in full first.

Few individuals have enough savings or liquid funds to enable them to purchase property outright. In countries where the demand for home ownership is highest, strong domestic markets for mortgages have developed.

Real Estate: is "property consisting of land and the buildings on it, along with its natural resources such as crops, minerals, or water;

immovable property of this nature; an interest vested in this (also) an item of real property; (more generally) buildings or housing in general. Also: the business of real estate; the profession of buying, selling, or renting land, buildings or housing. Residential real estate is a type of property, containing either a single family or multifamily structure that is then available for occupation for non-business purposes.

Residences can be classified by, if, and how they are connected to neighbouring residences and land. Different types of housing tenure can be used for the same physical type. For example, connected residents might be owned by a single entity and leased out, or owned separately with an agreement covering the relationship between units and common areas and concerns.

Title: Legal ownership in a property is created by the title to the property being transferred into a buyer's name. The buyer then obtains title when the seller of the property signs a transfer document which transfers the ownership of the property into the buyer's name. Once this occurs and the transfer is registered, the government land title office records will show that the buyer is the new owner. If and when anyone searches through those records it will recognize the purchaser as the owner.

Section 23, BC Land Titles Act: Effect of indefeasible title

23. (1) In this section, **"court"** includes a person or statutory body having, by law or consent of parties, authority to hear, receive and examine evidence.

(2) An indefeasible title, as long as it remains in force and uncancelled, is conclusive evidence at law and in equity, as against the Crown and all other persons, that the person named in the title as registered owner is indefeasibly entitled to an estate in fee simple to the land described in the indefeasible title, subject to the following:

(a) the subsisting conditions, provisos, restrictions, exceptions and reservations, including royalties, contained in the original grant or contained in any other grant or disposition from the Crown;

(b) a federal or Provincial tax, rate or assessment at the date of the application for registration imposed or made a lien or that may after that date be imposed or made a lien on the land;

(c) a municipal charge, rate or assessment at the date of the application for registration imposed or that may after that date be imposed on the land, or which had before that date been imposed for local improvements or otherwise and that was not then due and payable, including a charge, rate or assessment imposed by a public body having taxing powers over an area in which the land is located;

(d) a lease or agreement for lease for a term not exceeding 3 years if there is actual occupation under the lease or agreement;

(e) a highway or public right of way, watercourse, right of water or other public easement;

(f) a right of expropriation or to an escheat under an Act;

(g) a caution, caveat, charge, claim of builder's lien, condition, entry, exception, judgment, notice, pending court proceeding, reservation, right of entry, transfer or other matter noted or endorsed on the title or that may be noted or endorsed after the date of the registration of the title;

(h) the right of a person to show that all or a portion of the land is, by wrong description of boundaries or parcels, improperly included in the title;

(i) the right of a person deprived of land to show fraud, including forgery, in which the registered owner has participated in any degree;

(j) a restrictive condition, right of reverter, or obligation imposed on the land by the *Forest Act*, that is endorsed on the title.

(3) After an indefeasible title is registered, a title adverse to or in derogation of the title of the registered owner is not acquired by length of possession.

(4) Despite subsection (3), in the case only of the first indefeasible title registered, it is void against the title of a person adversely in actual possession of and rightly entitled to the land included in the indefeasible title at the time registration was applied for and who continues in possession.

Section 25, BC Land Titles Act: Protection of registered owner against actions for recovery of land

25 (1) In this section, **"courts"** includes a person or statutory body having, by law or consent of parties, authority to hear, receive and examine evidence.

(2) An action of ejectment or other action for the recovery of land for which an indefeasible title has been registered must not be commenced or maintained against the registered owner named in the indefeasible title, except in the case of

(a) a mortgagee or encumbrancee as against a mortgagor or encumbrancer in default,

(b) a lessor as against a lessee in default,

(c) [Repealed 2005-35-13.]

(d) a person deprived of land improperly included in an indefeasible title of other land by wrong description of boundaries or parcels,

(e) 2 or more indefeasible titles having been registered under this Act in respect of the same land, the registered owner claiming under the instrument that was registered first,

(f) a right arising or partly arising after the date of the application for registration of the title under which the registered owner claims, including, without limitation,

(i) the right of a purchaser claiming under a contract with the registered owner for the sale of the land, and

(ii) the right of a beneficiary if the registered owner is a trustee, and

(g) a right arising under section 23 (2).

(3) In any case other than those enumerated by way of exception in subsection (2), the production of a subsisting state of title certificate must be held in all courts to be an absolute bar and estoppel to an action referred to in subsection (2) against the registered owner named in the certificate, despite a rule of law or equity to the contrary.

Void instruments — interest acquired or not acquired

25.1. (1) Subject to this section, a person who purports to acquire land or an estate or interest in land by registration of a void instrument does not acquire any estate or interest in the land on registration of the instrument.

(2) Even though an instrument purporting to transfer a fee simple estate is void, a transferee who

(a) is named in the instrument, and

(b) in good faith and for valuable consideration, purports to acquire the estate,

is deemed to have acquired that estate on registration of that instrument.

(3) Even though a registered instrument purporting to transfer a fee simple estate is void, a transferee who

(a) is named in the instrument,

(b) is, on the date that this section comes into force, the registered owner of the estate, and

(c) in good faith and for valuable consideration, purported to acquire the estate, is deemed to have acquired that estate on registration of that instrument.

Section 29, BC Land Titles Act: Effect of notice of unregistered interest

29 (1) For the purposes of this section, **"registered owner"** includes a person who has made an application for registration and becomes a registered owner as a result of that application.

(2) Except in the case of fraud in which he or she has participated, a person contracting or dealing with or taking or proposing to take from a registered owner

(a) a transfer of land, or

(b) a charge on land, or a transfer or assignment or sub charge of the charge,

is not, despite a rule of law or equity to the contrary, affected by a notice, express, implied, or constructive, of an unregistered interest affecting the land or charge other than

(c) an interest, the registration of which is pending,

(d) a lease or agreement for lease for a period not exceeding 3 years if there is actual occupation under the lease or agreement, or

(e) the title of a person against which the indefeasible title is void under section 23 (4).

(3) Subject to section 49 of the *Personal Property Security Act*, a person contracting or dealing with, taking from or proposing to take from a registered owner, an estate or interest in land, or a transfer or assignment of an estate or interest in land, is not affected by a financing statement registered under that Act whether or not the person had express, constructive or implied notice or knowledge of the registration.

(4) The fact that the person who is contracting with, dealing with, taking from or proposing to take from a registered owner under subsection (2) had knowledge of a financing statement registered under the *Personal Property Security Act*, or that the person could have obtained knowledge of the financing statement by searching the personal property registry established under that Act, is not evidence of fraud or bad faith for the purposes of subsection (2).

GUEST CONTRIBUTOR
WINONA REINSMA

About the Authors:

George Greenwood

Since the beginning of 2003, George Greenwood has been facilitating seminars and investigating personal experiences concerning identity theft and issues involving privacy. The purpose of which is to educate on the act of prevention.

As the founder of Canadian Identity Resources Inc. and the creator of the "Keeping Identity Safe" Training programs, George has been providing programs designed to reduce people's risk and decrease their vulnerability to identity abuse, theft or fraud. There are specific programs designed specifically for individuals, families and business.

As an accomplished author, George Greenwood, prior to creating this *KEEPING IDENTITY SAFE SERIES*, George has written Five other books on the subject of identity theft: *"IN YOUR GOOD NAME: Identity Theft – A Canadian Perspective"*, *"CONFESSIONS OF AN IDENTITY THIEF"*, *"MEMORIES OF A STOLEN LIFE"*, *"NOW THAT I AM A VICTIM – WHAT DO I DO NEXT?"* and *"ID-TIPTIONARY"*

As a speaker, George Greenwood has addressed a wide variety of groups nation-wide, large and small – commercial and private. These engagements range from convention keynote speeches to facilitating local community seminars and workshops. Whether these programs are set for the Public, Chamber of Commerce Events or Business Group presentations, Civic Club or Church Group,

High School Classes or Community Policing Forums, George is pleased to deliver the message about this life changing, life damaging, horrific, yet non-violent crime, known as identity theft in a light-hearted way that all people can relate to and understand.

As an advocate, George has worked with Boards of Trade and Chambers of Commerce to produce resolutions to lobby both Provincial and Federal Governments into making changes in the laws affecting people's rights and the need for identity theft protection. George frequently meets with many Mayors, MLA's and Members of Parliament, including federal and provincial Cabinet Members, and officials of law enforcement. He was given the rare opportunity to address and present a submission of recommended changes to the Special Review Committee of the "Personal Information Protection Act" of British Columbia. Working with The Canadian Chamber of Commerce and Surrey Board of Trade, a resolution originally written by George was introduced to Parliament as S-4 and received Royal Ascent Oct 22, 2009. This was signed and included into law on Jan. 8, 2010 as section 402.1, placing ID theft into the Criminal Code of Canada.

Other advocacy issues include: photographs on our Health Cards, mandatory and uniform electronic receipt truncation laws, practices in the way debit and credit numbers are then printed, disclosure laws so businesses must inform customers of data losses, and the creation of an identity theft victims' registry.

In these roles, author, consultant, speaker and

advocate, George Greenwood has been well received by various media, in the format of numerous newspaper articles, radio talk shows and news clips on both radio and television across Canada.

Canadian Identity Resources Inc. is designed to work with business owners and upper management to uncover ways that their business could be vulnerable to abuses from identity thieves. The KEEPING YOUR IDENTITY SAFE Seminars are used to teach the public the need for increased awareness based on prevention. Pro-action vs. re-action.

George Greenwood's personal mission and purpose is to impact the lives of people by teaching that identity give-a-way is more prevalent than identity theft. We must all accept the responsibility to do more to reduce our risk and decrease our vulnerability by changing those habits that impact the personal security of the information entrusted to us.

Author, Keynote & National Speaker, Trainer, Consultant & Identity Abuse Prevention Advocate

To order more copies of this book and series or other books by George Greenwood...

Please go to our website:
    www.keepingidentitysafe.com.
Click on either tab: On-line purchases or Mail purchases.

You can also email us at:
    george@keepingidentitysafe.com.

Our desire is to reduce your risk and decrease your vulnerability so you can always be.
The ONLY YOU there is!

Canadian Identity
Resources Inc.

As the author of this book series, I personally want to thank Winona Reinsma for her collaboration on this book project. Her dedication to detail and for her ability of digging for accurate information has been amazingly helpful. I would not have been able to do it without her. Winona's knowledge of the mortgage and real estate industry, including how it all fits together to effectively work is impeccable.

Winona started her career in the financial world right after high school. Having worked for several Credit Unions and as an Assistant Manager for Canada Trust, she has seen many changes in the industry.

Her experience includes Financial Planning, real estate, mutual funds, stock market trading, advanced mortgage strategies, small business, and fundraising.

After 18 years working for financial institutions, she became an independent Mortgage Broker, a personal financial strategist and a retirement expert. Winona's mission is to empower her clients so they can make informed decisions
through education, market analysis, and alternative options.

Winona's helpful and winning attitude is her best attribute. She will be glad to tell you, in her own words..."I love working with my client's, always in their best interests, providing new solutions or a better way to finance their dreams."

Professionally, Winona enjoys facilitating her own

Financial Empowerment Workshops. Where she teaches financial strategies, and is a personal coach for clients wanting to change their financial paradigm.

Winona is also active in her community. She is a Director for Critter Care Wildlife Society, Associate Coordinator for Valley Women's Network Langley Chapter, and Secretary for Senior's Connect.

Mortgage and Finance expert, Advocate for animals, seniors and woman's issues

Thank you, Winona, for working with me on this book...
Without you...
I could not have written it.

George Greenwood

Watch for other books included in this series as they are published.

Contact me by e-mail:
george@keepingidentitysafe.com
to be informed of their release.

Notes or Questions:

Made in the USA
Charleston, SC
04 February 2017